THE TOKYO CHRONICLES

日
記

ALBERT L. SIEG
with

STEVEN J. BENNETT

omneo
An imprint of
OLIVER WIGHT PUBLICATIONS, INC.
85 Allen Martin Drive
Essex Junction, VT 05452

THE TOKYO CHRONICLES

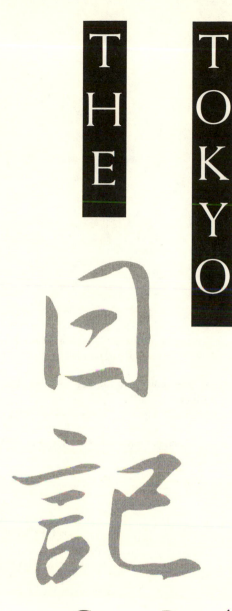

*An American Gaijin Reveals
the Hidden Truths of
Japanese Life and Business*

Oliver Wight Publications books may be purchased for educational,
business, or sales promotional use. For information, please call
or write: Special Sales Department, Oliver Wight Publications, Inc.,
85 Allen Martin Drive, Essex Junction, VT 05452.
Telephone: (800) 343-0625 or (802) 878-8161; FAX: (802) 878-3384.

Library of Congress Catalog Card Number: 94-076392

ISBN: 0-939246-70-8

Text design by Marysarah Quinn

Printed on acid-free paper.

Manufactured in the United States of America.

1   2   3   4   5   6   7   8   9   10

Dedicated to

My wife, Irma, my daughters, Karen, Diane,
and Susan, and my granddaughter Leanne—
three generations of inspirations

CONTENTS

CONTENTS
viii

CONTENTS

ix

CONTENTS

x

ACKNOWLEDGMENTS

In a sense, the subtitle of this book is misleading; the hidden truths I reveal are far more than the experiences of one American *gaijin*. The book actually reflects the influences, teachings, and observations of the many people, both Japanese and American, whom I worked with and learned from during my seven years in Tokyo. In recognizing those people and honoring them for their contribution to the book, I fear that I'll surely leave out some who deserve mention and thanks. So in Japanese fashion, I offer my sincerest apologies to those people in advance.

Back in 1984, I set out for Tokyo with three compatriots from Rochester, New York to launch Eastman Kodak (Japan): Dave Biehn, Jim Mills, and Howell Hammond. We were joined shortly thereafter by Jerry Curnutt. I'm deeply indebted to these members of the "gang of five," each of whom was willing to undertake the Japan assignment. Their help and guidance were crucial to the success of our fledgling Japanese enterprise. Over the next five years, thirty more people from

Rochester joined us, and each made significant contributions to our collective efforts. My thanks to this entire group for their commitment and spirit of adventure.

More difficult to enumerate are the many Japanese whom I came to know as friends and very patient teachers. Toshio Nakano proved himself invaluable as a mentor, confidant, and translator, and with his bilingual skills and cross-cultural understanding made it possible for us to undertake many of the negotiations that we conducted with Japanese companies. The three presidents of our largest affiliated companies—Takuya Sawada, Tsutomu Kimura, and Kohenosuke Suzuki—were also key players in Kodak Japan's rise to success. My thanks to each of these people for being part of the board of the company and for their exceptional guidance and counsel.

Others in Japan also deserve my sincerest thanks for their patience and help. They include Yasuharu Nagashima, our legal advisor, Akita Aoki, our Japanese patent attorney and close friend who did more than anyone else in helping me understand the culture of the Japanese business world, and Masae Kazama, who for seven years struggled to teach me the Japanese language.

Special thanks go to Aki Hioki, my secretary and assistant. Her bilingual and cross-cultural skills bailed me out of many potentially embarrassing moments and helped me maneuver through day-to-day life in a society so very different from my own. Her willingness to teach me about Japanese mores and etiquette made it possible for me to blend into the culture as much as a foreigner can.

I'm also grateful for the support from Kodak's home office in Rochester. Colby Chandler, Kay Whitmore, and Phil Samper deserve a great deal of credit for choosing to pursue a Japan strategy in the first

ACKNOWLEDGMENTS

xii

place, and I thank them all for the unswerving support during my tenure in Tokyo.

Another key player I would like to thank is Steve Frangos, a friend, neighbor, and former colleague who not only played an important role in establishing Kodak's first manufacturing facility in Japan, but also introduced me to Jim Childs, publisher of Omneo/Oliver Wight Publications, Inc. Jim was instrumental in developing and refining the book, and linked me with Steve Bennett, a professional writer who was able to craft my stories into a form that I hope will appeal to a broad range of readers. Special thanks go to Steve's family for allowing us so much of his and their time while we worked on the manuscript.

Finally, and most important, I couldn't have undertaken this book project without tremendous support, patience, and assistance from my wife, Irma. She not only filled in many of the holes in my re-membrances of people and events, but her own insights from living abroad for seven years have brought a wonderfully fresh perspective to the book. Thanks for your keen eyes and good memory; this book is a tribute to your experiences as well as my own.

INTRODUCTION
Dial 119

Except that they [the Japanese] do not walk on their hands instead of their feet, there are few things in which they do not seem to have been impelled in a perfectly opposite direction.

—Sir Rutherford Alcock,
*   Britain's first diplomatic representative to Japan*

If you walk around downtown Tokyo today, it would appear that the Japanese had reversed their trajectory since Sir Alcock's time. What with people wearing Western-style clothing, modern skyscrapers dotting the downtown areas, and familiar fast-food restaurants—Kentucky Fried Chicken, McDonald's, Arby's Roast Beef, and Shakey's pizzas, to name just a handful—you'd think you were

actually in any metropolitan city in the States. The Western traits are best summed up by the discovery of an eight-year-old Japanese boy during a family visit to Anaheim, California: "Look, Dad, they even have Disneyland here!"

Yes, they have Disneyland in Tokyo, too. But if you move beyond the outward signs of Westernization, you'll quickly notice a number of distinctions between Japanese and Western culture, the kind that led Sir Alcock to conclude that the Japanese are not like us at all. In fact, in some ways the Japanese are a mirror image of us.

They drive on the left, while we drive on the right. They start at the back of a book and read from right to left, while we start at the front and read left to right. They use their last name first, and first name last; we do the opposite. They dial 119 for emergencies while we dial 911 for the same. They call strikes and balls in baseball, while we call balls and strikes.

Where it would be possible to expand this list of surface differences for many pages, there are plenty of deep-seated issues that separate the Japanese from the Western world, in general, and the United States, in particular. These have to do with fundamental differences in our economies, our attitudes about work, the emphasis we place on human relationships, and the like.

In the next few years, an awareness of these cultural and economic differences will be critical; many experts believe that Asia and the Pacific Rim countries will play a substantial economic and political role in the twenty-first century. And it's generally agreed that Japan will be a keystone in the Asian countries' rise to power. Yes, the recession of the early 1990s severely weakened the Japanese economy, but it would be naive to assume that Japan can't muster the driving

spirit that enabled it to quickly rebuild after World War II and become a vibrant global economic force.

Unfortunately, it's very difficult to get a sense of Japan from the many academic and business books that have been written on the country and its people. And Japan has never been accorded the same kind of emphasis that Europe has in our school system. As a result, Americans tend to be ill-informed and often misinformed about Japanese history, society, and business. Because of the general lack of knowledge about Japan, American businesses often find it particularly difficult to navigate through the cultural terrain and are often frustrated by what they perceive to be impenetrable boundaries or discriminatory policies and practices. And without knowing which "buttons" will make Japanese consumers want a product, how to tailor a product for Japan (products that sell well elsewhere in the world may have to be completely reformulated or packaged for the Japanese), what the game rules are for tipping the playing field in their favor, and how to motivate the government to really help companies make inroads into the distribution system, they're likely to become frustrated and pack up shop after a brief foray. Which is sad because they'll forgo an enormous market for their products or services.

In this book, I've tried to document the key issues that American businesspeople need to know when they set up shop in Japan or try to build a national presence there. Rather than organize the book according to conventional chapters, I've chosen to share my experiences in Japan through a collection of stories that chronicle my experiences as the president of Kodak Japan, the U.S. subsidiary of Eastman Kodak that markets and distributes a full line of photographic products,

conducts research and development into electronic imaging, and manufactures a variety of photographic products.

I was sent to Tokyo to launch Eastman Kodak's Japanese operations after I demonstrated to the company that Japan was the second largest market for photographic goods in the world and that our position there was deteriorating at an alarming rate. As I reported to the chairman at the time, Walter Fallon, if we didn't take swift and strong action, Kodak would be out of the consumer photographic business in Japan within several years. In addition, we'd let our arch rival, Fuji Photo Film, build up a safe haven in its home country with virtually no challenge from Rochester. Fallon's successor, Colby Chandler, than asked me to go to Japan and build a business from the ground up—a challenge I couldn't resist.

We started in Tokyo with a handful of Americans and Japanese, and when I left, Kodak Japan had more than 4,000 employees, a state-of-the-art R&D facility, and several manufacturing sites. To "jump start" Kodak Japan, we engaged in a strategy of aggressive mergers and acquisitions, at one time controlling more than forty companies involved with various aspects of photographic film distribution and electronic imaging research. Eventually, we consolidated the company into one primary company, of which I served as president, and three subsidiaries, each with their own Japanese president at the helm.

My seven years in Japan proved to be the high point of my career. I'd already been with Kodak for twenty-eight years, having started as a research chemist and then working my way through various positions until I became a corporate vice president and the director of strategic planning worldwide. But none of my previous experience could have

prepared me for the shock of running a business or living in a culture so fundamentally different from my own.

Much of what I'd read in academic books on Japan was either too general or too theoretical to be helpful on a day-to-day basis; some was completely off the mark. And none of the books I read really taught me the nitty-gritty of succeeding in Japan as an individual and as the leader of a foreign capital company. I resolved early on that at some point I'd pass on to others what I had learned, so they could avoid the kind of potholes I encountered in my efforts to blend into the culture as much as possible and to help my company achieve its full competitive potential.

The stories in this book represent the subtle and hidden bits of inside advice and information that I wish I'd had when I first came to Tokyo. They're based on my experiences as both a visitor to Japan and as the head of a U.S. company that successfully broke into the fast-paced Japanese photographic marketplace.

I offer the information in the stories neither as a Japan "basher" or a Japan apologist, nor as an official spokesperson for the Eastman Kodak Company. My chronicles are simply the reflections of a *gaijin* (foreigner) who was lucky enough to have good support and understanding from his Japanese colleagues and friends and extraordinary support from his home office. Also, I do not pose my observations as iron-clad truths; it is a mistake to view the Japanese as a monolithic culture in which everyone thinks and acts the same. The Japanese do have strong cultural traditions that create a tendency for people to think and behave in certain ways. But there are so many individual variations on age-old themes that it's dangerous to view them with a "one-size-fits-all" mentality.

I believe that the insights and observations in my stories will be helpful for anyone who does business in Japan or deals with Japanese companies as a supplier or buyer, or as a partner in some kind of business alliance. And for those who are interested in Japanese culture for its own sake, I think that the everyday experiences that my wife, Irma, and I had will shed some interesting light on how people live in a society that seems so Western on the surface but is so very different in terms of basic perceptions of the world.

Finally, I hope that this book will help all readers to appreciate and celebrate the unique qualities of a country that will undoubtedly have a critical shaping force in the world economy of the next decade and beyond. With that in mind, I now present the details of seven years of business intrigue, good friendships, and a new appreciation of our own role in the world today.

Albert L. Sieg

Rochester, New York
June 1994

THE TOKYO CHRONICLES

日
記

DO YOUR BEST!
Understanding the Japanese Work Ethic

The human traffic jam on Mt. Fuji seemed to get more dense by the minute as the serpentine path to the top narrowed and twisted back on itself. As I paused to rest for a moment—the thinness of the air was becoming apparent—I sighted an elderly woman dressed in a country skirt and blouse scurrying up the path in her sneakers like a world-class climber. Under the brim of her straw sun bonnet I could see deep lines in her face, telling of many years on the mountainside. Despite her age (which I'd guessed was at least eighty), she was remarkably sprite and energetic. Her agility was all the more amazing given the heavy wooden crate strapped to her back. She paused for a moment when she saw a foreigner on the path and called out to me earnestly: "Gambatte! . . . Do your best!" She then continued her rapid clip to the food kiosk on the sixth level to unload the bottles of beer and other supplies in her backpack.

An old Japanese saying has it that everyone should climb to the top of Mt. Fuji once but only a fool does it twice. I did it three times (during visits from my daughters, so I'm not sure what that makes me). The mountain looms 12,600 feet tall and can be seen clearly from Tokyo, sixty-five miles to the northeast. The Japanese have revered the mountain for hundreds of years, often referring to it as Fuji-*san*, *san* being the honorific form of *Mr.* or *Mrs.* Sometimes they personify it as the "shy lady" because the peak is often enveloped in a layer of wispy clouds and hidden from sight.

Every year, tens of thousands of people make their way to the top; for many, the trek is almost a calling. And while there are no official restrictions on climbing the mountain, the Mt. Fuji Climbing Association strongly urges people to make their ascent during July and August; during the rest of the year, the paths are covered with snow and ice and can be extremely dangerous.

So the mountain is abuzz with activity from the middle to the end of the summer, when people throng to the parking area. To make it easier for the average person to climb (a volcanic mountain, Fuji rises straight out of the ground with no foothills), the government has created nine rest stops from the base to the peak, with a roadway wide enough for cars that ends at the fifth. Most people park their cars at level five, which is about 40 percent of the way up to the top, then continue on foot to the peak (because of the crowds, you still might have to walk more than a mile to reach the level-five path).

Along the way to the top, climbers stop at various levels to rest their legs or purchase refreshments at the kiosks or rent a space to lie down. Sometimes the rest areas look like a sea of humanity, with people jammed together head to toe on their *tatami* mats. The rest

areas have another important function as well: documenting your ascent. When you start off, you purchase a wooden walking stick that might have a bell or pennant as an ornament at the top. As you reach each level, you can pay to have your stick branded with a hot iron, officially marking your climbing achievement and rite of passage to the top.

Back in the old days, before the roads leading to levels one through five were built, everyone started at the base, making the climb an all-day adventure; from level five, the ascent takes about five hours. (I'm told, however, that a few purists still insist that the only way to climb Fuji-*san* is from the bottom.) While it's a little over a mile from level five to the peak as the crow flies, the path constantly twists and turns and switches back on itself. Although the climb never requires pitons or other technical gear, a few spots along the way require hand-over-hand action. Still, thousands of people, ranging from toddlers to the elderly, make the trek every year. Beyond level seven, where the path is reduced to a width of just three feet (compared to a breadth of thirty feet at the lower levels) people have to wait their turn to budge an inch. The traffic jams become worse when the path going up coincides with the path going down, and climbers have to walk in single file.

The top of Fuji consists of a crater a quarter of a mile in diameter and is often jam-packed with throngs of people. Many of the people who make it to the top camp out overnight so they can watch the sunrise, which the Japanese consider the quintessential Mt. Fuji experience. Some prefer to camp out on levels seven and eight because the temperature at the peak can drop below freezing even during the summer.

DO YOUR BEST!

The view from the top is truly breathtaking—and humbling. If the clouds aren't too thick, it's possible to see straight across to Tokyo and to the Pacific Ocean, across farms and rice fields, cities and towns, and the Five Lakes near the base of the mountain. It's no wonder that the gracious mountain has such a strong attraction for Japanese and foreigners alike.

Like so many other things in life, going down Mt. Fuji is a lot easier than going up. At some points the path to the base coincides with the ascending path, and the going is slow. But at other points, it follows a more direct route, and some people choose to take the express method: sitting on a piece of cardboard or heavy plastic and sliding down the pea-sized volcanic cinders, many of which have been worn smooth from erosion and heavy foot traffic.

As people making their descent pass fellow hikers making their way to the top, they'll often call out "*Gambatte!*" to urge them on. I was exhorted to "do my best" on the way up because I was a *gaijin*: I later found that Japanese often say *gambatte* to foreigners when they meet them in the woods, on tours of shrines, and in other public places. It's almost as if *gaijin* need to be reminded of the fact that in Japan there's little trust in providence; so the Japanese will never wish anyone "good luck." In fact, there is no Japanese word for *luck*; it's up to each individual to make things happen to the best of his or her ability.

Though it might seem extreme to Westerners, the *gambatte* mentality is almost a Japanese version of the Puritan work ethic. Deeply ingrained throughout the entire culture, it certainly served the Japanese well as they dug their way out from the ruins of World War II and made their spectacular climb to become a major force in today's global economy. In everyday life, *gambatte* means endurance in the face

of great pain or defeat. People might ultimately fail at an endeavor, but there's no stigma—*as long as they've tried their best.*

In business, *gambatte* means never giving up, forging ahead even if the company doesn't meet its sales or profit targets: when managers send their people on the road, they exhort them to try their damnedest. *Gambatte* also means never resting on one's laurels; rather, it means relentlessly plotting one's next moves to ensure forward movement toward a goal. That's how to reach the top of the mountain!

When you climb Mt. Fuji, never ask how far it is to the peak—that would be an admission of weakness. When you do business in Japan, just push on until you reach your goal, doing your best every inch of the way.

DO YOUR BEST!

7

ON BEING NUMBER ONE

The Japanese National Passion for Superlatives

"Sieg-san, we've decided to take a one-week vacation,"
Tanaka-san said to me with a big smile on his face.
Hinoki-san grinned and nodded his head.

This was music to my ears; I'd been prodding
Tanaka-san and Hinoki-san for two months to cash in some
of their earned vacation time. I was told that in many
Japanese companies people accumulate vacation days but
simply don't use them. Since these guys were working for a
Western company, perhaps they'd behave a little more like
Westerners and take a much needed break.

"Great!" I said. "Where will you go?"

"To Hawaii."

"Why's that?"

"Because it's the number one vacation spot for Japanese
people to visit."

One is the most important number in Japanese society. Whatever you do, strive to be number one—*ichiban*. Whatever you buy, strive to purchase the number one item in its class. Wherever you go, make it the number one place. And whenever you talk about Japan and its people, talk about the number ones—like the fact that the Tokyo Tower is taller than the Eiffel Tower.

The *ichiban* mentality has been the driving force in Japan since the end of World War II, when the single, unified goal became to surpass the West in every conceivable measure. The overwhelming drive to be number one energized industrial Japan and catapulted the country into a position of economic leadership. While the recession that began in the early nineties has slowed Japan's ascent, *ichiban* still dominates the psyche of most Japanese, and the quest to be number one shapes people's lives from the moment they can walk. I got a firsthand dose of *ichiban* while walking down the hallway of our office building one day. I couldn't help but overhear a conversation between two women employees, one of whom had just returned from maternity leave.

The new mother was explaining that her little boy would end up working for the number one government agency. But in order for him to be eligible for such a prestigious position, he would have to get into the number one university, Tokyo. In order to get into Tokyo U, he would need to graduate from the number one private high school, which in turn would require being graduated from the number one middle and elementary schools. And of course, to get into the number one elementary school, he would need to be graduated from the number one preschool. "Wow," I said to myself. "The kid's still in diapers, and he's already got the rest of his life's challenges plotted out for him!"

The Japanese government tends to fuel the quest to be number one—and disdain for achieving anything less—by publishing lists such as the most desirable companies for the current Japanese graduating class. In the early eighties, the list was dominated by auto makers. In the mid-eighties, it shifted to electronic companies. And in the late eighties it became popular to work for companies like banks and financial institutions. Whatever companies were in the "number one" category would always be flooded with an onslaught of applications. Given the fact that the Japanese introduce themselves with their company affiliation—"Kodak *no* Sieg *desu*" (I am Sieg from Kodak)—being with a number one company can take on great social significance.

Businesses, too, talk about the "biggest," "bestest," and "mostest." At some level, the claims can get artificial and meaningless. For example, we were in no way the number one photographic company in Japan in terms of sales and revenues; that distinction clearly belonged to Fuji. But we skirted the issue by saying that we were the number one photographic company in the world. Or we'd segment the market by saying that we were the number one professional *imaging* company in the world, or we were the number one in medical imaging worldwide.

Any company, no matter what product it makes or service it offers, could make some kind of number one claim to fame. I was particularly amused by a pencil company that announced it was the "number one producer of *red* pencils"!

While this might seem peculiar to Westerners, the drive for *ichiban*—being number one—has resulted in some remarkable product developments, such as the smallest tape recorders that can possibly

be built, the Walkman and Discman, and now the DAT portable tape recorder.

But the drive to achieve the exalted rank of number one can have devastating effects on people if they "only" achieve the number two slot. Consider the 1994 Winter Olympics when figure skater Midori Ito, a native of Japan, competed against Christi Yamaguchi, an American of Japanese descent. Midori was so devastated at coming in second to Yamaguchi that she publicly apologized to the country for letting everyone down and then gave up her amateur skating career.

Another sporting event story also illustrates the darker side of *ichiban*, this one from the annals of Japanese baseball. For years, the Tokyo-based Yomiuri Giants dominated the Japanese baseball league. When I was working in Japan, the team was managed by the famous Sadaharu Oh, who hit fifty-five home runs a season when he had played for the Giants in the 1960s and 1970s. During one tense game, the Giants faced the Hanchin Tigers, which had two Americans on the team, including the spectacular batter, Randy Bass (each Japanese team can have as many as two foreigners). Bass, who was one home run shy of Sadaharu's old record, had three or four more games to play before the season ended. Rather than risk losing the status of being able to boast that their manager held the number one home-run track record in the league, the Giants intentionally walked Bass (who never did go on to meet the record).

For Westerners, the *ichiban* mentality can seem daunting: How can you compete in a country whose people are totally preoccupied with being number one in everything, including your market niche? The fact is, foreign companies can actually harness the *ichiban* energy to create better products and services.

For example, when we set out to improve the quality of our work in Japan, we decided to undertake some of the quality circle activities we'd read so much about. Everyone in the company participated in a quality circle during the lunch hour or after work. Our employees defined the problems, assembled "fishbone" charts, worked on the problems, and then reassessed the situations to see if any improvements took place. We then encouraged the circles to enter a competition to see whose improvement was number one. Every six months we went off site and had each group make a ten-minute presentation. A group of three or four judges—outside quality circle consultants that we'd hire—judged the presentations. The winner received a "president's trophy" (meaning I had to buy it). The competitions were taken extremely seriously and probably spurred the innate Japanese drive for top quality even further.

We also sponsored interdivision golf tournaments with a series of prizes that epitomized the *ichiban* mentality. There was, of course, the number one prize for the best score. There was also the prize for the number one worse score (what would be called the "booby prize" in an American tournament). Not surprisingly, these prizes were offered not only for the entire game but for the first and last nine holes as well!

"We try harder" is unacceptable; being first is all that counts.

SIGN WARS
Attack and Counterattack

Visions of Dorothy and Toto swept through my mind as I braced myself against the stiff winds battering the roof of the eight-story office tower in Ginza. As president of Kodak Japan, it was my duty to accompany the Shinto priest to the top while he blessed our new neon sign. When he finished the ceremony, I flipped the switch and we were instantly bathed in the warm yellow light that we all associated with Kodak and its products.

When my colleagues first proposed spending the equivalent of hundreds of thousands of dollars on a neon sign, I thought I'd entered the twilight zone. But a quick trip to the Ginza section of Tokyo at night convinced me that we should make the investment. The hundreds of giant corporate neon signs atop the six- to eight-story buildings in

Ginza create a fantastic scene of color and form—and to be part of that light show is to be part of the Japanese business landscape. So I authorized the project, not realizing that the placement of a sign is not only an important way to boost awareness of our company name but also a shot fired in a competitive volley with our arch rival, Fuji Photo Film.

I was told that our sign would be matched by their sign, only their sign would be directly across the street, slightly taller, or slightly anything that satisfies the itch to be number one. Then we'd have to respond in kind. Such leapfrogging is the essence of Japanese competitive strategy, and it's done in a way that resembles the ancient Asian game of Go. In Go, two players sit on opposite sides of a gameboard that consists of adjacent squares and move their pieces (stones in the old days) both to gain control over as many squares as possible through attack and counterattack and to isolate the opponent from any future moves.

In business, Japanese firms are also constantly attacking and counterattacking to gain control of as much market share as possible. They move with astonishing speed to seize new opportunities or respond to competitive threats, even in markets where they have no prior experience or track record. Consider what happened to Procter & Gamble when it introduced disposable diapers in Japan in 1977. At the time, babies in Japan wore cloth diapers, and mothers washed them at home. P&G instantly owned the marketplace through its initial attack, since it didn't have to contend with a single competing Japanese product. But while P&G continued to sell its entry-level product, a number of Japanese companies, such as Kao and Unicharm, were busy inventing their own versions that were better suited to the physique of

Japanese infants and offered innovative features such as elastic leg bands and thinner, more absorbent materials. By 1985 the Japanese firms had nearly wiped P&G off the map with its counterattack, reducing the giant's consumer product market share to 5 percent.

Procter & Gamble subsequently counterattacked the counterattack by incorporating the Japanese innovations along with some of their own, making products more appropriate for Japanese babies, and by the early eighties regained another 20 percent of the market. The Japanese diaper makers responded in kind with more incremental improvements, and the game of "Diaper Go" continues to this day.

At the other end of the alimentary tract, McDonald's had a similar experience when it placed its first golden arches on Japanese soil in the 1970s. Pundits predicted that the Japanese palate was too refined for burgers and fries, but the new food became an instant hit, especially with the younger crowd. *Hamburger* (pronounced the same as in English) became a permanent entry in the Japanese lexicon and a staple in the Japanese diet.

This was music to McDonald's ears, which attained the enviable position of sole provider in a booming market—but not for long. Within several years at least ten Japanese burger chains, including Lotteria and Mos, dotted the landscape with fast-food joints offering their own version of the Big Mac, such as the Teryaki Burger. Interestingly, McDonald's countered the Japanese companies by offering their own "Japanified" fast-food innovations, such as a variety of fish sandwiches.

In our business, we felt the constant need to attack and counterattack every day in order to contain and keep ahead of Fuji. Soon after

we'd set up operations in Japan, Fuji's president, Onishi-*san*, made the stakes of the global competition with Kodak clear: "We are in a race for survival with Kodak. And now we can almost see their numbers [that is, the numbers on the backs of the runners in the road race]."

Fuji translated Onishi-*san*'s marching orders into relentless attacks and counterattacks, matching us on pricing and the introduction of new photographic products, and even following us into new business areas. Fuji and Kodak went head-to-head in the copier market. When Kodak began marketing clinical blood analyzers, Fuji did so as well. About the only thing Fuji didn't do was acquire a drug company as Eastman Kodak did. That bit of prudence saved Fuji from having to disentangle itself from an expensive nonphotographic venture—as Kodak began to do in 1994.

It was interesting that even though Fuji was already a household name, it felt compelled to counterattack our efforts to become better known in the consumer marketplace—even through the placement of new neon signs. Now, sign wars can be an expensive proposition, given the cost of constructing the signs and renting building tops. In our case, the initial construction costs were especially high because Kodak's corporate yellow color was hard to duplicate electrochemically. It took a couple of months of experimentation and modification of the gases and pigments in the glass tubes to create the right shade.

The framework for the signs is also a considerable undertaking, involving massive steel girders capable of supporting fifty-foot mazes of glass tubing during high winds and stormy weather. Since the signs are deemed construction projects, they are blessed by a Shinto priest before the work begins in order to purge evil influences that could cause accidents (construction workers won't pick up a hammer until

the purification ritual has taken place) and again during the actual placement to ensure that the deities residing in the materials are appeased and that the construction area is safe for others to enter. The president of the company is expected to participate in the rituals, which take place regardless of the weather. I'll never forget that windswept evening atop a building in Ginza when I was sure we'd all end up as two-dimensional displays on the pavement below, or the sign placement ceremony that took place during a major snowstorm in Sapporo.

Whatever your sign says, the choice of the building on which it will sit is critical; unless it's in a prestigious location with good visibility, your investment will be wasted. Part of the game is demonstrating how much money you spent on picking a great site. We spent six months scouting out a building for our first sign in Ginza, the most elite business area and heavily trafficked section of Tokyo. We finally found a soon-to-be-available building at the main intersection. It would be harder to find a more prestigious spot in the city—perhaps in all of Japan!

We then went through several months of negotiations with the landlord, which included an evaluation to make sure that we were the type of "sign tenant" he'd want. When we finished the rental agreement, the landlord informed us that he'd just leased the property to Waco, one of the top department store chains in the country. Waco's management told us that the building didn't suit its needs, so we'd have to wait while they demolished it and constructed a new one. It shouldn't take more than several years—four, at most—before we could put up our sign, they said.

We weren't about to wait three or four years to place our first sign, so we found three other locations—Shinjuku, Osaka, and Sapporo. I balked at Sapporo, the northernmost island of Japan, because it seemed a bit out of the way. My colleagues insisted that Sapporo was a terrific place for our sign, however, because it had the highest elevation of all the islands. "We would then be able to say that we have the highest sign in all of Japan," Sawada-*san*, one of our Japanese presidents, exclaimed. How could I argue with that?

When we finally did get our original sign erected at the building in Ginza (four years after our agreement with the first landlord), we unanimously decided it was worth the wait. From the ground, the glowing yellow Kodak box floated distinctively in the air, unlike any other signs on the Tokyo roofline. But it was joined several months later by a bright green box bearing the Fuji logo, right across the street. Not to be outdone, Fuji had cut a deal with the landlord of the building facing ours and had moved with lightning speed to construct and place a neon sign of its own. "I bet they measured our sign and made theirs an inch higher," I thought out loud when I first saw Fuji's sign. Oh well, with Sapporo unchallenged, at least we could claim the tallest sign in the entire nation. For now, anyway. . . .

Never rest on your laurels after introducing a new product or innovation; you can be sure that an impressive counter-maneuver is just around the corner.

THE TOKYO CHRONICLES

KODAK GO
Breaking into the Japanese Marketplace

The crowd of media people gathered on the eighteenth floor of the Kasumigaseki Building in downtown Tokyo gasped as Sawada-san, one of our Japanese presidents, pulled back the drapes covering the windows of the reception suite. Just hundreds of feet away, an enormous airship bearing Eastman Kodak's flaming red logo and name hovered motionless in the air as if suspended from the clouds by invisible strings. The business and financial reporters cheered with delight and then clapped their hands before barraging us with questions about our plans for the airship, what it cost us to rent it, maintenance costs, where we housed it, and scores of other details that would make for good copy.

Sawada-*san* and I breathed a sigh of relief at the enthusiasm of the reporters and the apparent success of the media event. We'd called the press conference a week earlier but didn't say what it would be about—just that Kodak had an important announcement. That was anomalous enough in Japanese media circles to pique the curiosity of a sizeable number of reporters.

The press conference proceeded in typical Japanese style, which entails two or three speakers getting up and making a presentation, after which the sponsors serve food and drink. Our plan had been to keep the drapes closed until the airship pilot, with whom we maintained contact via a two-way radio located in another room, could "park" the craft outside the building and position it for the most dramatic effect. Unfortunately, turbulence slowed the ship's speed to a crawl, and Sawada-*san* was forced to ad lib about Kodak Japan's technical achievements and plans for expanding into the Japanese marketplace. The reporters grew restless as Sawada-*san* intoned on about Kodak's plans, clearly aware that they hadn't yet heard the "important announcement." The tension building up in the room only added to the reporters' excitement at the appearance of the airship beside the office tower.

Had the stunt failed, it would have diminished our credibility with the Japanese media and cast a pall over future media events. The gamble and expense were well worth it, though: the press conference launched what turned out to be several years of profitable, high-flying media excitement.

Our blimp adventure began when Susuna Tanaka, the president of the Japan Airship Service (JAS), approached me about Eastman Kodak's sponsoring his company's airship, the only one licensed to fly in

all of Japan. I suspected that he'd already made an offer to our major global competitor, Fuji Photo Film Company, but that Fuji declined because of the exorbitant price tag—several hundreds of thousands of dollars per year with a three-year exclusive contract. Fuji also probably figured that it was safe to pass up JAS's offer because we wouldn't be crazy enough to accept it either.

A flash of "sticker shock" did hit my gut, but I quickly realized that the blimp could help us achieve one of our primary goals: to convince the Japanese that we were committed to making a go of it in their marketplace. We knew that perceptions about our commitment to Japan would be a critical factor in our success there. After all, Japanese consumers don't buy products; they buy *companies*.

To establish Kodak as a great company—the kind of company that people would want to buy from—we planned to sponsor various sporting events. We also built a new R&D laboratory, which sent a critical message to the marketplace. If we were willing to invest in one of the country's most scarce and precious commodities—land—and then back up that investment with mortar and brick, we were certainly here to stay. Our "digging roots" contrasted sharply with the tactics of many European and American companies that take a six-month "winger" in Japan, then pack up and leave if they don't experience instant success. No wonder that so many Japanese are distrustful of foreign firms!

We further bolstered trust and confidence by listing our shares on the Tokyo Stock Exchange. While some experts claim that listing a foreign company on the Exchange is a waste of time, we reasoned that trading our shares in the local economy would send a strong signal of intent to our constituents, keep our name in front of the financial community every day, and make it easy for our employees to get

involved with stock purchasing plans. These advantages could help us overcome the hiring difficulties that so many Western firms encounter because of the Japanese people's reluctance to stake their employment on firms that may be here today, gone tomorrow.

A Kodak-sponsored airship would add the perfect finishing touch to our commitment campaign: it would be a splendid reminder of how serious we were about having a strong presence in the Japanese marketplace. Unfortunately, the price tag exceeded Kodak Japan's budget, so I had to figure out a way to get top management of the U.S. operations to share the burden. That proved to be relatively easy; all I had to do was raise the specter of the 1984 Summer Olympics in Los Angeles, when Fuji outbid Kodak for the sponsorship in the photographic category, breaking Eastman Kodak's twenty-five-year tradition as official film sponsor for the games.

To add insult to injury, Fuji flew a bright green blimp festooned with its logo over the Olympic stadium and across the entire Los Angeles area. Top Kodak officials savored the thought of flying our own airship over Seoul during the 1988 Olympic games, and within a few days of my request, a plan had been worked out that would enable other parts of Kodak to help pick up part of the tab. Japan Airship's Tanaka was surprised but nonetheless delighted that we'd agreed to sponsor the blimp, and he worked out a leasing arrangement that would cover us through the upcoming games.

While getting permission from the Korean government would take about a year and a half, we had a good head start because Kodak Japan had won a contract for developing a custom, electronic imaging system that would be used to create the identification badges worn by the Olympic players and personnel.

In the intervening months, we spent as much time as the weather would permit doing practice flights with the airship, which we named *Kodak Go* (*Go* means "ship"). Ironically, even after we stopped flying the blimp, *Kodak Go* became widely used as the term for "airship," just as *xerox* and *kleenex* have taken on generic meanings here. As the Olympics approached, we began wending our way toward the "silicon island," Kyushu, at the southernmost tip of Japan.

The 600-mile trip took three days, since a blimp can only go as far as its ground crew can travel in 24 hours. We also had to carefully select landing sites along the way; it's not easy to locate a suitable space in Japan for something that dwarfs a Boeing 747. From Kyushu, we would fly 100 miles across the Sea of Japan to the shores of Korea, then press on to Seoul.

The plan called for *Kodak Go* to arrive about a month before the games, so that we could do practice runs around the stadium and train our Korean ground crew. But we never made it beyond Kyushu. About the time of our arrival, unrest between North and South Korea flared, and the South Korean government feared that an airship flying around Seoul, which was less than forty miles from the border, would make a splendid target for North Koreans who wished to disrupt the games. We could still fly in Seoul's air space, the government said, but only if we agreed to use the television cameras with which *Kodak Go* had been outfitted for the games to search for covert actions near the border. There was even talk about arming the ship with air-to-surface weaponry.

We declined the offer and, deeply disappointed, headed back to Tokyo, where we would continue to use *Kodak Go* to increase our name recognition and demonstrate our commitment to Japan. In particular,

KODAK GO
25

we wanted to use the airship to increase awareness of Kodak among younger film buyers, so we targeted our flights over large assemblages likely to attract young people, such as sporting events and *matsuri* or festivals.

We flew whenever the weather was conducive to airship flight; a blimp requires almost perfect conditions, with minimal ground winds. A small layer of snow on the body of the airship will neutralize the craft's lift capacity, a factor that eliminated the possibility of flying over much of the country during the winter. Tokyo was relatively snow-free, so it made a good year-round flying location. It was also the home of Fuji's corporate headquarters, which made the air space even more appealing. Located in a low-rise residential section of the city, known as Aoyama, the twenty-eight-story Fuji Tower stuck out like a sequoia tree on a freshly mowed lawn, begging to be buzzed. To the anger of Fuji officials, we frequently did just that—maintaining the airship within legal limits, of course. Forays into Aoyama were particularly satisfying, especially since Fuji had done the same to us after the 1984 Olympics when it flew its airship cross-country to Rochester, New York and made frequent passes over Kodak's corporate headquarters.

On one occasion, I was allowed to co-pilot *Kodak Go* until we reached metropolitan air space. While I'd had previous hot-air ballooning experience, I wasn't at all prepared for the amount of effort required to navigate the blimp. I pushed and pushed on the rudder, working up quite a sweat, yet nothing seemed to happen. Then, all of a sudden, the nose suddenly jerked up as if it had been slammed by a tidal wave, and I had to work hard to compensate for my overzealous rudder actions.

I quickly learned that flying a blimp requires a good deal of patience, not unlike the mindset that's required when breaking into the Japanese marketplace. Like *Kodak Go*, the Japanese marketplace exhibits extraordinary inertia and resistance to *gaiatsu*—outside pressure. *Gaiatsu* can refer to a foreign competitor or government. Such outside influences are troubling because the driving force in Japanese business and society is a sense of internal harmony. *Gaiatsu* upsets the status quo, causing "difficulty" or "confusion" within the Japanese business community.

Fuji responded to *gaiatsu* from Kodak by seeking permission from the Japanese government to fly its own blimp for six weeks during the New Year holiday, when millions of people in Tokyo are out and about visiting various temples and shrines. Not surprisingly, the government responded by granting Fuji special permission to fly its airship in Tokyo air space for the holiday, alongside *Kodak Go*. Fuji deployed its closest airship for the mission, one located in Germany. Since time was of the essence, the company chose to deflate the blimp, fly the shell to Tokyo, then reinflate it, making the mission a costly one (probably close to half a million dollars' or more for the whole venture).

By December 1989, Fuji's blimp joined *Kodak Go* in what became Japan's biggest media sensation of the decade. Ironically, most of the media interest in Japan was triggered by television, newspaper, and magazine coverage abroad. Back in the States, a *U.S. News & World Report* article featured the two blimps engaged in "air wars" over Tokyo; when taken from a helicopter and with a telescopic lens, photographs of the two craft made it seem as if they were within inches of each other. In reality, they were never less than a mile apart. The drama caused by the distortions, however, was priceless. We were besieged

with calls from reporters around the world about the death-defying air battles reportedly taking place every day. One Tokyo station even interviewed me about the size of the hole likely to result from one airship ramming the other: Would it be big enough to cause the damaged craft to plummet to earth?

The media attention continued until Fuji's permit expired and the company withdrew its airship back to Europe. At the time, we experienced a minor setback in our blimp program that, in the end, turned out well for us. Our deal with Japan Airship allowed the company to use *Kodak Go* to train pilots when we weren't busy roaming the countryside or buzzing Fuji Tower. During one training flight, a new pilot ascended too steeply and dragged the tail on the ground, damaging the rudder and ripping a fourteen-foot gash in *Kodak Go's* cloth-laminate shell. The crew attempted to gain enough altitude to turn around and land, but quickly discovered that it had no control over the steering mechanism and that the blimp could fly only in ever-decreasing concentric circles. So there was nothing to do but wait while *Kodak Go* lazily spiralled downward. The pilot came within ten feet of successfully landing the craft in a farmer's field, but the docking rope became tangled in nearby power lines, flipping the ship upside down and allowing the remaining helium to escape. When the engines finally stopped, *Kodak Go* had been reduced to a pathetic, limp balloon draped over the high-tension lines.

Miraculously, no one was injured by the crash. And since no bodily harm or property damage had come of the incident, the Japanese government deemed it a "heroic emergency landing," with no need for official inquiries. Even so, *Kodak Go* was damaged beyond repair, and we lost nearly three months while Japan Airship replaced it.

On the positive side, though, the press coverage of the crash again catapulted Kodak into the headlines.

Our new airship was equipped with considerably more powerful turbine motors than its predecessor, enabling the craft to carry nine people instead of six. This was a definite plus, since we were barraged with requests for rides in the blimp and often granted them to important commercial customers and reporters. The new *Kodak Go* was adorned with a picture of a carp—a symbol of strength—that ran from nose to tail. The name *Kodak* was painted beneath the fish, creating an unforgettable sight for miles around.

We flew the new *Kodak Go* for nearly a year, until our contract with Japan Airship Company expired. JAS offered us an attractive new vehicle if we wanted to continue, one equipped with an electronic message board and flood lamps for night flights. But we concluded that we'd already received a tremendous return on our investment. We'd forced our primary competitor to take expensive and drastic action to defend what it had considered to be a safe haven and to divert resources that it could have applied elsewhere in the world. We gained invaluable press coverage that would have otherwise been impossible; foreign companies rarely receive the kind of attention we garnered through our blimp escapades. And most important, we proved to the buying public that Kodak had the patience to become a serious photographic force in Japan, one that was in it for the long haul.

Patience is more than a virtue; it's an essential ingredient of success.

KODAK GO

29

I AM SIEG FROM KODAK
The Social Life of the Company Man

Kimura-san looked horrified when I told him that I declined an offer to play golf with our largest customer. "You can't do that, Sieg," he said with a pained look on his face.

"But I can't play," I protested.

"Doesn't matter. We'll go out to the driving range and give you some practice."

A week later I called back the customer and set up a golf game. I also told him I was a "bit rusty," which he seemed to accept at face value—that is, until the day of the big game arrived. It started off badly. By the ninth hole, my score was a stinging 128; with nine more to go, I could perhaps set a world's record.

"Gee," I thought to myself. "If I could just swap my golf and bowling scores, I'd be a world-class pro at each!"

One of the things I most looked forward to about returning home was never having to play golf again. But in Japan I wasn't "civilian Sieg"; I was "Sieg from Kodak," which meant that I had significant social responsibilities on behalf of my company.

In Japan, the relationship of a person to his or her company is almost as strong as familial relationships, so it's not surprising that most of a working person's social life is very much connected with the company, especially for those working their way up the corporate ladder.

As the most senior officer of the company, I was expected to participate in a tremendous number of social activities, ranging from golf games to private dinners at restaurants and drinking sessions in bars or cabarets. Not surprisingly, social drinking and entertaining is a major industry. According to the Japanese government, in 1993 the country spent more on business entertainment than on education or defense. This statistic is all the more telling given the fact that business entertainment is not tax-deductible for companies with revenues of more than 5 million yen ($5,000), so companies must feel it is a vital business function.

The tendency for Westerners is to avoid intensive business socializing: they don't want to casually spend a lot of company money, or to overstep company guidelines about expense accounts. But you soon find out that entertaining is an essential element of doing business in Japan and not something just done for pleasure. My Japanese cohorts strongly urged me not to look like I was above or against business entertainment, and to authorize the necessary expenditures. I did. And I became more comfortable with business socializing after I was convinced that it was possible to establish a reasonable range for our outlays.

Once in a great while when entertaining a top-tier customer we'd go all out to a dinner at an elegant Japanese restaurant where it was easy to spend $300 to $500 per guest. Add in the cost of a round of drinking and cars to take the guests home, and the tab could run $1,000 a head.

Far more often, we'd do the "B" version and go to a restaurant that specialized in business entertainment. At the Imperial Hotel, for example, we were able to spend between $100 to $200 a head for a quality meal. Best of all we could charge our entertainment to a house account, which meant that the restaurant would simply bill the company once a month for food and drink. This was a very impressive thing to do, since only prestigious "regulars" would be allowed to have such accounts.

Other than sponsoring and attending dinners for special guests, I became comfortable with the idea of spending money on very elaborate New Year parties so that customers would feel as if they were part of the Kodak family. The all-you-can-eat-and-drink bashes would take place each year during the first week in January, in the cities where Kodak's major customers were located: Tokyo, Osaka, Sapporo, Nagoya, and Fukuoka. This meant flying from city to city to entertain a total of 1,500 guests. But the intangible payoffs were well worth it.

Rather than sitting at the tables with the guests at each New Years bash, our staff would circulate throughout the room, thank all of the customers for their business during the past year, and express their hopes for even more business the following year. (After everyone had left, we'd eat and have a party of our own.) My senior Japanese managers explained that this was the way you build strong and lasting "family" relationships.

In addition to coordinating business entertainment, the top company man is expected to engage in social sports—golf, unfortunately, being the preemptive game of choice among Japanese businessmen. Generally, the idea is to play nine holes, have some food and drinks, then complete the remaining nine holes. Not surprisingly, the final nine holes are often a bit "looser" than the first. (My game was so bad that I would stop counting after the tenth hole; I could never figure out which club to use, and the caddies, who normally provide expert advice, didn't speak English.) In any case, there was never any business talk on the links, just general socializing and the building of business friendships.

One would think that with the tremendous amount of time spent on social entertainment, the spouses of businessmen would be involved as well. Because she was an American, my wife, Irma, was occasionally invited to business dinners and generally had no qualms about joining us. The first time, however, she did feel conspicuous being the only spouse at our table. On the Japanese side, it's expected that wives will tend to the housekeeping, the children, and the calculator: women often play the role of household chief financial officer. It's fairly common for Japanese men to turn over their paychecks to their spouses and receive an allowance. But it is uncommon for women to accompany their husbands on business forays to restaurants, bars, and cabarets.

Since the board of Kodak Japan was half Japanese and half American, I thought we might be able to bend tradition a bit and once a year invite the board members, with their wives, to a corporate dinner. The Americans agreed that it was a great idea, and the Japanese members didn't indicate that we'd broken any major cultural barriers. Their

wives graciously received the invitations but didn't anticipate that they were actually expected to come to the event.

Things begin to change, though, after several more attempts to bring the board members' spouses into the social fold. Sawada-*san's* wife, Fusako, was the first to join us, which wasn't surprising since she had lived in Germany for a number of years. The next year, Tomiko, the wife of another Japanese Kodak president, Kimura-*san*, came to a dinner, and the following year Nobuko, the wife of the third Japanese president, Suzuki-*san*, joined us as well.

In addition to making the dinner more fun, our "unusual" attitude about spouses reinforced an important signal that we wished to give the rest of the country: while Kodak Japan was indeed a Japanese company, it was a Japanese company with a distinctive Western streak. That streak was consistent with the realities of doing business in Japan as a foreigner. *Gaijin* always have their feet in both camps, and the art of succeeding in Japan is to find a comfortable bridge between the two.

Yes, I was Sieg from Kodak. But I never forgot that I was Sieg from Rochester, too.

What counts is not who wins the game of golf, it's whether or not you took the time to play.

I AM SIEG FROM KODAK

OF GREAT
HARMONIZERS AND
MELODIOUS LEADERS
The Role of the Company President

It's not essential for the superior, including the man at the top, to be intelligent. In fact, it is better if he is not outstandingly brilliant. If his mind is too sharp and he is excessively capable in his work, the men below him lose a part of their essential function and may become alienated from him. To counterbalance the dependence on the leader on the part of the followers, it is always hoped that the leader in his turn will depend on his men.

—Chie Nakane, *Japanese Society*

Written in 1970 by a professor of social anthropology at the Institute of Oriental Culture of Tokyo University, this work is frequently quoted to help Westerners understand the Japanese business mind. Much of what's said in *Japanese Society* still rings true. Not about the Japanese presidents' intelligence: many are indeed "outstandingly brilliant." But their role doesn't call for devising brilliant strategies or insights into the marketplace or creating new visions for where their companies might be tomorrow. Nor does the Japanese president (*shacho*) run the business on a day-to-day basis. Rather, a *shacho's* job is to be a "great harmonizer" who binds the workforce together. Most Japanese presidents say that they spend at least 50 percent of their time on personnel and human relations issues. And while doing so, they rely on the rest of the organization to run the company on a daily basis and create long-term strategic plans.

The presidents of Japanese companies are regarded with great esteem. Someone named Kato would be called "Kato-*shacho*," rather than the common honorific, "Kato-*san.*" They're also revered for their age, as most have achieved the position in their late sixties or early seventies. (In general, the Japanese equate age and wisdom, so when a person under fifty achieves a major position in government or industry, it's front-page news. No wonder that the Japanese are so curious about youthful business and government leaders in the United States!)

Presidents are almost always selected from within the company and are chosen for their ability to be good listeners, guide others, and serve as father figures. They're also people who have survived the winnowing process; while their counterparts have been retired at fifty-five, future presidents have the talent and expertise to go on to serve on the company's board and often achieve its highest position (human

relations manager) before moving on to the presidency. Since only extremely capable people are asked to join the board, there is an element of meritocracy in the selection process.

All this is clearly very different from the role of presidents in U.S. companies, and as I quickly learned, when Americans assume the position of *shacho* in a U.S. subsidiary based in Japan, they often find themselves caught between two conflicting worlds. On the one hand, the Japanese expect you to take on the characteristics of a Japanese president—father figure and all. They also expect you to draw on your networks with suppliers, other heads of companies, government bureaucrats, and so on, which, of course, you can't do because you didn't go to college in Japan. On the other hand, senior executives in your parent company expect you to lead the subsidiary as you would an American firm—standing at the helm and spending your time making key strategic decisions that filter down through the chain of command. So you're pulled and stretched by two diametrically opposed forces.

Over time, I felt more comfortable in my role as I learned to create a hybrid executive style that seemed to please everyone most of the time. I maintained a strong hand in the day-to-day operations of the company, but also went to far greater lengths to mingle and get to know my people than I would have in the United States. During many afternoons I sat in the conference room outside my office drinking tea and chatting with suppliers, employees, customers, and people from the media. While this was painful at first—high-level operational issues, I thought, should dominate my time—I eventually learned to enjoy the role of listener and "provider of wisdom."

I also became accustomed to a great deal of party life; as president,

I was expected to help plan and host major parties for customers, suppliers, university professors, and key reporters. My wife, Irma, and I also accepted as many party invitations as we could, although we could have gone to at least one party a week during our stay in Japan if we had the time or energy. In addition to helping me fulfill my presidential obligations, the parties were a great way to build networks and compensate for the fact that I came into the country with no connections whatsoever.

As Sieg-*shacho*, I did some serious socializing with my immediate Japanese subordinates. Normally, the subordinates would have been working with their president for many years, so interpersonal connections would have been firmly in place. But I was a total stranger from a culture so alien to theirs that I just as well might have beamed down from another planet.

How could I break the ice with my group? I once put this question to a Japanese president I'd gotten to know, and he said, "Easy. Go out and do a lot of *karaoke* singing with them."

Panic shot up my spine like a *tsunami* wave: I'd been told that my singing voice had the tonal quality of a garbage disposal digesting a steel fork. Surely there were other avenues to presidential success that didn't involve singing—perhaps checkers or cards (I eventually learned to play golf, since much of the mingling and chatting with prestigious guests is done on the links).

As fate would have it, after a party we gave for ten of our top customers, the group unanimously insisted that we all visit a well-known *karaoke* bar. *Karaoke* literally means "empty orchestra." You select a song you'd like to sing from an official song book, and the *karaoke* machine plays a laser disc with the music. The laser disc also

projects images related to the music on a jumbo screen, so the singer becomes part of a multimedia performance.

"Great!" I said, figuring that I'd simply decline to sing if asked. Surely, after explaining my tonal impairment, no one would insist on listening to my crooning, let alone allow it to be amplified throughout the entire bar.

The small, smoke-filled bar was crammed with people who took turns drinking and picking up the microphone for a song or two, often demonstrating exquisite vocal qualities. About a half hour, and several rounds of beer and *misuwari* (whisky and lots of water), my group began insisting that I, too, take up the mike. I'd had enough liquor to feel relaxed and less inhibited—but certainly not enough to induce me to sing for the crowd. It soon became clear, though, that my protests and disclaimers were being written off as polite attempts at humility and that refusing to sing was simply not going to be an option for me. With sweat beading up on my forehead, I began flipping through the bar's song book in search of a tune I actually knew (the bar had one English and one Japanese book). I pointed to my choice, "I Left My Heart in San Francisco," and made one more feeble attempt to convince my compatriots that their ears would probably never be the same after my performance.

Alas, it was to no avail. *"Gambatte!"* (Try your best), everyone shouted from the table.

I did try my best, and for a few moments I became totally absorbed in the dazzling scenes of the Golden Gate Bridge and other images of San Francisco being projected on the screen in the front of the bar. When I finished singing, I received a standing ovation, which made me think that perhaps the performance wasn't as bad as I thought—

until my interpreter leaned over and said, "Sieg-*sacho,* you truly *do* have a terrible voice!" He then proceeded to explain that the louder the audience claps, the worse your performance; the bar patrons are actually awarding you "emotional points" for doing something that's obviously painful.

Whatever the reality of the applause, I made the rite of passage and demonstrated that I was a good sport and willing to participate in the off-hours entertainment so important to my group. I also accompanied my people on many more *karaoke* outings. Strangely enough though, I was never asked to sing again.

The successful gaijin *business leader shakes hands like a Westerner and bows like a Japanese.*

TRICKLE-DOWN MANAGEMENT
Leaking Information from the Top

Of all the festivals that I attended in Japan, the rites held at the Sensoji Temple was by far my favorite. One of the most unusual things about the Asakusa Compound, where the temple was housed, was the quarter-mile open-air mall shrouded by an enormous steel superstructure that could be closed during inclement weather. Inside the mall were stalls for every souvenir and gadget imaginable. Normally, the thirty-foot-wide street in the mall bustled as shoppers browsed from stall to stall. But during the festival, which was held in honor of the deity residing in the temple, you could scarcely move because of the wall-to-wall crowds. From a gaijin's perspective, it was worse than a Ginza subway ride at rush hour.

The dense crowds, however, didn't stop a group of fifty or sixty people from carrying out the traditional activity of

*hauling an enormous portable shrine through a mile-long route
around the streets so that the deity who normally resided in the
temple could tour the town. The secret of moving the shrine
through the throngs of people: good management on the part of
the portable shrine leader.*

A lot of American literature on Japanese business leaves you with the impression that all decisions are initiated by middle managers and then developed through a consensus process. In this model, upper management supposedly waits for the decisions while thinking about how to best entertain top customers. Based on my observations, I don't believe that upper management in Japan is so complacent that it would allow all decisions to emanate from the middle. While many decisions may originate with the middle or bottom echelons, I think that the most important decisions are formulated at a high level and then filter down through the ranks of the *bucho* (division heads) and the *kacho* (section heads). The catch is that top management's decisions aren't formalized; instead, they're posed in subtle ways, eventually making their way down through informal channels of communications.

The portable shrines or *mikoshi* nicely illustrate the concept. The *mikoshi* is an elaborately decorated miniature wooden temple (six by four feet) mounted on a framework of timbers eight inches in diameter. As many as twenty to thirty people on each side are needed to lift the 2,000-pound shrine and carry it from the temple throughout the town, often on a route that extends a mile or more. In some cases there's a competition involving two teams that vie to see whose *mikoshi*

can be first to break through the crowds and return to the spot where the deities in residence begin their tour.

Whether the event involves one or two teams, it's critical to have a good route plan that considers how to maneuver through the crowd, how to deploy your best people in terms of strength and stamina, how to monitor people and bring in replacements when necessary, how to pace the forward movement to a group chant, how to decide who will serve as an "advance team" to arrange the crowd to make way for the shrine so that no one gets trampled, and other key logistical issues.

Now, to an outside observer, it's often not clear who's calling the shots; the *mikoshi* just seems to "know where to go." Yet there is clearly someone making decisions because you'll often see a second group of men and women stepping up to relieve the original crew in an orderly fashion. Without a good plan and strong cooperation, the *mikoshi* trip would be a disaster.

In business, as in the *mikoshi* rites, it's often difficult for a foreigner to figure out exactly who's in charge. Yet things do get done. If the leader says, "X is the outcome I desire," then everyone will figure out a way of supporting X. I discovered this principle of trickle-down management midway during my stay in Japan when Kodak acquired a Japanese film processor and two Japanese marketers of photo supplies. While these companies would give us a terrific jump start in the Japanese marketplace, their administrative, sales, and marketing functions would have to be consolidated. We didn't ask the companies to pass out pink slips to any of the 4,000 employees involved; we wanted them to reorganize their workforces so that redundant positions would be eliminated and productivity enhanced. I was sure

TRICKLE-DOWN MANAGEMENT

45

that the presidents of the three companies would respond with an equitable plan that benefited the whole organization. To my naive chagrin, though, the request for consolidation led to a series of counterproductive discussions about whose staff should prevail.

One of the reasons that consolidation proved to be extremely difficult was that the three companies had very different histories and cultures. At our first meeting, the leader of the company with the longest history and highest revenues claimed that the redundant functions and necessary redeployments were the problems of the other two acquisitions. He also argued that his company should be the "head" acquisition because its people had attended the most prestigious schools. One of the companies was smaller and had less stature, but its president nevertheless argued that it should have a major say in its future. The third company, largely blue collar, simply didn't want to have a consolidation plan forced down its throat.

I made another mistake when I assumed that by the second meeting—or even at subsequent meetings—some progress would be made. But each time, we came back to the same points, the same arguments, and the same defenses. It was almost as if none of the previous meetings had taken place! Just when I was beginning to think that the melding of the acquisitions was a mistake, one of my senior staff people said to me, "Sieg-*sacho*, you have to tell them what the goal is you're trying to accomplish. Once they find that out, they'll work on the 'how' and find a way to make it happen through the consensus process."

My mistake, he explained, was making a free-form request at the initial meeting, when I said, "We have three companies and excess staff, and we need to find a way of dealing with that excess. Work it

out." Ironically, in trying *not* to be a typical American boss—in not delineating a specific goal—I thought I was inviting the Japanese business leaders to use the decision-by-consensus process described in all the textbooks. What I should have done instead was to say, "This is what I want: a single company that consolidates all three of your organizations and eliminates redundant staff functions. You figure out how to do it in an equitable way that makes the most sense for Kodak Japan."

When top levels of management let the desired outcomes be known, everyone works hard to arrive at a plan that supports the outcomes. I suspect that much information passed through the ranks via what I call the "latrinonet"—casual conversations that occur in washrooms, in hallways, and around the water cooler, and when people are making tea and engaging in other informal activities. Consensus really occurs around these impromptu discussions, and feedback flows up and down the chain of command.

An important element in the consensus-building process is the *nemawashi,* or "binding roots." Just as it's necessary to prepare the ground for planting a tree, it's necessary to prepare people and make them receptive to accepting a new idea and, ultimately, to committing to a decision. The *nemawashi* might take place during a meeting or during an evening drinking stint at a bar. Either way, the roots must be bound before everyone will sign off on the *ringi-sho,* a document that marks the culmination of the decision-making process. The *ringi-sho* contains all of the pertinent information about the issues at hand, along with the final decision. Everyone who participates in the decision affixes his *hanko* (stamp) to it. (Signatures are meaningless in Japan. Instead, people use their personal *hanko,* which is officially

registered with the government, to stamp mortgage and other key documents. *Gaijin* are allowed to use their initials.)

The overall decision-making process in Japan, from the "leak from the top" to the *ringi-sho,* can be painfully slow, compared to the Western-style process. But once everyone has agreed on how a goal will be achieved, decisions can be executed with lightning speed because there's no need to "sell" the decision: everyone has already bought into it, and the tight hierarchical structure makes it easy for marching orders to filter down through the chain of command.

By contrast, when a high-level group in a Western company makes a decision, it still has to convince research and development, manufacturing, and marketing to support it wholeheartedly, so it may be some time before a new idea actually sees the light of day. Whatever the merits of the Japanese approach to decision making, it's different enough from most Westerners' experience that it can be baffling and frustrating; it's not clear who's actually making the decision. Nothing seems to happen, but then suddenly everything runs at full tilt, and the goal of the leader is implemented very quickly.

This seems to apply whether you're running a major corporation or a *mikoshi* ritual. The first time I attended the *mikoshi* ritual in Asakusa, I stood on a fence and held onto a lamp post so I could take pictures. (I later learned the Japanese usually take small ladders with them when they know they'll be stuck in human gridlock so they can get a better view.) From my vantage point, I could clearly see the *mikoshi* team moving through the crowd with incredible ease. Wherever the *mikoshi* went, a hole would open in the sea of humanity and then seal itself up as if it hadn't been disturbed at all. But most amazingly, it seemed to be happening without anyone's being in charge. "How does everyone

know where to go?" I asked my friend incredulously. "And who's in charge?"

My friend smiled and said, "Sieg-*san*, the better the *mikoshi* leader, the less he's distinguishable from the rest of the team. What you do see is his will reflected in each footstep that the team members take on their journey to the temple."

The successful business leader has the ability to implant solutions in other people's minds—and takes no credit for the ideas.

GURUPU
United We Stand

When Michael Anderson walked up to the bowling shoe rental stand and asked for a size thirteen, the clerk looked as if she'd just dropped a 16-pound ball on her foot. She stared at the six-foot six-inch, 230-pound American, then said, "Chotto matte" (wait just a moment), as she ducked into the office. A moment later she reappeared with the entire office staff, which gazed at the gaijin's gargantuan feet and giggled in unison (by Japanese standards, a size five would be considered quite large).

After several minutes of chattering with her peers, the clerk went over to the rental sign and yanked off a display shoe, which just happened to be a size thirteen, then disappeared once again and emerged with its mate, which she held up in the air in triumph. The bowling staff cheered and we got on with our game.

Twice a year we'd take our entire staff on a group outing, which by popular consensus would often start at a bowling alley. Everyone would then break up into small groups and go on to a bar or *yakatori* place for a few beers (*yakatori* are small pieces of chicken grilled over charcoal fire on a six-inch stick). From there, smaller groups might go on to yet a third party for a final round of drinks.

It would not be overgeneralizing to say that people in Japan have a strong affinity for groups (pronounced *gurupu* in Japanese). Many anthropologists believe that the group culture in Japan is a remnant of the country's long history of rice farming. Rice is grown in fields flooded one at a time, starting with the field at the top of the slope. The flooding requires a tremendous amount of interdependence; each farmer must know when the flooding will take place so he can prepare his rice in hothouses ahead of time. Because of the need for constant communication, the farmers tend to live close to each other, surrounded by the rice paddies.

That spirit of interdependence seems to have permeated all aspects of Japanese life, including business. As a result, Japanese businesses tend to be group-oriented, rather than an accumulation of individuals. Just walk into a typical Japanese office space and you'll see few private offices. People tend to work at large tables and engage in a tremendous amount of communication, rather than the nose-to-the grindstone work that takes place in individual cubbies of U.S. companies. People tend to wear uniforms, or uniformly dark suits, creating a very homogenous appearance.

As a Westerner, I found this group mentality to be both a plus and a minus. On the one hand, I realized its immense power; on the other, I often felt the need to back off and "do my thing." While I do consider

myself a team player, my years in a Western company had taught me where to draw a clear line between my own activities and those of my colleagues. In Japan, the line blurred and often disappeared, and I constantly fought the urge to redefine it. I quickly learned that I wasn't going to be able to lead a Japanese staff from an armchair; my job was to create a group environment and serve as a magnet for group activities.

Fortunately, my Japanese colleagues were patient with me, and even forgave me for my gaffs, such as the time I announced my plans for presenting awards to the top quality circles in our company. (Despite our small size, we had about fifty quality circles; even the office workers formed a QC group to improve routines such as the routing of mail and messages.) I'd purchased trophies, had the names of the groups engraved on them, and told Sawada-*san* and Kimura-*san*, two of our presidents, about my plans for singling out several people from the groups when I announced the winners. Both men looked pained, and Kimura-*san* told me that it would be a "big mistake, Sieg-*san*. In Japan, we don't single out individuals from the group. It would cause the person a great deal of embarrassment and harm the group feeling."

Does this mean that there are no individualists in Japan? Of course not; Japan boasts many fine artists, musicians, intellectuals, and, contrary to popular mythology, even some entrepreneurs. Many Japanese also study abroad, and children of Japanese businessmen on overseas assignments often get a dose of the individualism inherent in Western-style schools. In fact, some children who have studied abroad become so out of synch with the Japanese school system that they need to complete their education at the American School in Japan. (When I

left, about 30 percent of the students in the American school were Japanese.)

Even so, the group dynamic far outweighs individual expression in most aspects of Japanese society and business, and Westerners must often make an effort to adjust to the group mentality. Interestingly, many of the team-oriented concepts that Westerners had high hopes for importing, like quality circles, have been very disappointing, and a number of American companies have announced their plans to abandon them. In my opinion, Americans don't understand that you just can't take an idea like quality circles out of its cultural context and overlay it on a culture that has exalted the individual since the pioneer days. This isn't to say that concepts like quality circles *can't* work in the United States; to the contrary, just about any idea can be adopted if you first "condition the soil" through education and training and develop solutions to likely problems before they're actually needed.

For Americans who plan to live in Japan and lead companies there, the need to understand the Japanese cultural biases against individualism is critical. Otherwise, they won't be able to acquire a sensitivity to, or at least an appreciation for, *gurupu*. That sensitivity is essential for becoming an effective "harmonizer," which is the chief role of the Japanese leader. For in Japan, harmony in the group is the major pathway to success on any project.

Successful foreign capital companies harness the power of the group dynamic while gently nurturing individual contributions.

THE TOKYO CHRONICLES

A VISIT WITH THE MAYOR OF YOKOHAMA

Buying Land or Renting Space in Japan

The wind whipped up the normally calm sea in Yokohama Harbor, transforming it into a white-water river. Irma and I had all we could do to keep from getting seasick while trying to socialize with the mayor of Yokohama's entourage. Fortunately, we succeeded on both counts; after all, Kodak had a great deal riding on this little harbor cruise late in September 1989.

Soon after my arrival in Japan, we announced plans for building a state-of-the-art research laboratory that would develop new semiconductors and other materials crucial to our future in the digital imaging market. And while the procurement of land in the United States can be a relatively straightforward process, land is an extremely precious and scarce commodity in Japan. (The Japanese population, which is about half that of the United States, lives in an area the equivalent in size to 4 percent of the state of California.) That scarcity makes the acquisition of any parcel an intensely competitive affair, particularly in the business communities of the major cities. If a company is willing to head to the rural areas, it can acquire land with less difficulty, but then it runs the risk of not being able to find employees willing to make the commute, especially if train service is limited or nonexistent.

To help us through the intricacies of finding and securing land, we decided to retain a "land acquisition consulting service" to work with our internal real estate expert. These consulting services are popular in Japan, which isn't surprising given the difficulty of locating land that meets your needs.

Our consulting firm, a subsidiary of the Fuji Bank, recommended five or six areas that would be appropriate for siting our new research facility. After visiting the possible locations, we all agreed that the Kohoku New Town area of Yokohama, twenty miles southeast of Tokyo, would be a good choice for us.

It was close enough to Tokyo that we could attract the kind of high-level employees we were seeking, yet far enough away that we wouldn't be paying Tokyo prices. At the time, Kohoku New Town land sold for 600,000 yen per *tsubo* (about 33 square feet), making the cost (about $100 per square foot at the time), compared with more than $25,000 per square foot for the most expensive space in Tokyo. The town of Yokohama promised to extend subway service into Kohoku New Town within ten years, but in the meantime we would be able to bus people to the facility from the nearest train station (about twenty minutes away).

Most important, seven acres of land, an unusually large parcel to come by in such a desirable location, was up for grabs.

The development plans for Kohoku New Town included various business and residential sites, as well as a high-tech center, so we would fit right into the scheme of things. But that alone wouldn't guarantee us the land. We'd first have to fill out an application, along with the twenty or so other companies that wanted to build at the site.

Our consultants not only helped us find the Yokohama parcel and coached us through the application process, but they established the appropriate contacts with the Kohoku New Town Land Development Center (LDC), a local government council that would decide which company would be chosen to be the new resident of this area of Yokohama.

The consultants also provided me with invaluable insights about the art of making a land acquisition. Unlike in the West, where land goes to the highest bidder, generally irrespective of who the bidder might be, land prices are fixed in Japan. Decisions about who gets to buy land are based on who the contenders are—that is, whether they'll be good neighbors who are willing to "promote friendly relations." So the art of being chosen as a land holder rests in maximizing your appeal as an applicant.

Upon the advice of our consultant, we engaged in a great deal of relationship building, such as going out for drinks with the manager of the Kohoku New Town development; inviting the LDC staff to our offices for tours; and, short of revealing confidential strategies, giving them; in-depth information about the nature of our business and our long-term plans. Because we were planning to build a laboratory on the site, we also had to answer lots of questions about the chemicals that we planned to store and use. Given the close proximity of schools and residential housing, the regulations were incredibly tight, and we had to work hard to build a high level of confidence that we'd be able to comply with the laws and procedures.

Over the next several months, we held a series of meetings with the Land Development Center to discuss our application. Initially, the meetings were very formal, involving my research director, a few members of his staff, and several key LDC people. At this stage, the meetings were what the Japanese would describe as "dry"—the Western style of doing business, which involved getting down to brass tacks about the transaction at hand. The meetings then became "wet," with the discussion shifting to the intangibles, such as what kind of neighbors we'd make and whether we could sustain friendly relations. As in virtually all Japanese transactions, when it comes to land deals, human relations are ultimately the basis on which all decisions are made.

Our presentation apparently succeeded in convincing the LDC that we were sincere about developing excellent relations. We received an official phone call informing us that the Center had whittled down the candidates to five finalists and we were among those chosen for final consideration. That meant it was time for an official visit to the mayor of Yokohama. While the Kohoku New Town LDC was an autonomous body, our land acquisition consultant made it clear that the mayor had a great deal of clout in deciding who would be allowed to break ground in his area.

The mayor was a thin man in his late seventies, and he was not in terribly good health. At the time of our first meeting, he was too ill to come to work, so we met with the deputy mayor. Early in the applica-

tion process, our land acquisition consultant had briefed me about the purpose of the meeting with the mayor, should it happen—namely, to give the mayor's office a sense of what kind of people we were. So for an hour we sipped tea and talked about everything under the sun— except Kodak.

Following the meeting, our real estate man struck up a chatty relationship with the Land Development Center, and a month later we were invited for a harbor cruise with the mayor's office and the LDC staff. I didn't think that the stiff wind would bother the sixty-foot tour boat, but the water splashing on the windows gave us an indication of what was to come as the boat left its mooring. The tour boat's main passenger area resembled a Japanese conference room with its *tatami* mats and low tables. Long benches ran the length of the room just under the windows.

The Land Development Center had arranged for a professional tour guide (and interpreter) to explain to us about the details of each boat and dock in the harbor, and despite the choppy water, the entire experience was extremely pleasant. Between descriptions of the sites, the director of the Land Development Center asked many questions about our personal lives and what it was like to work in America. Once again, the purpose of the meeting was to build friendly relations rather than to wheel and deal and focus on contractual issues.

Another few weeks passed after the harbor cruise, and our real estate director received a call requesting another visit with the mayor. His contact also "leaked" the information that the Land Development Center was very interested in developing Yokohama as an international center and that Kodak's application had been selected. The information "leak" was intentional and typical of many official transactions. It's often said that nothing is ever a surprise in Japanese business; you always go to a meeting knowing what's been decided. The real purpose of the meeting is for everyone to look at each other and say, in effect, "Yes, we're going to do this."

So off we went to visit with the mayor of Yokohama, who, we were glad to see, was feeling up to meeting with us personally. We sat in low overstuffed chairs facing the door, which is the traditional orientation for guests. The mayor began with some small talk, then turned the meeting over to an official from the Land Development Center, who welcomed us as new residents of Yokohama. The official then said that in order to extend our relationship, the city of Yokohama would donate 100 cherry trees to the city of Rochester, New York. The meeting then adjourned, with no talk about the next step in the purchase of the land; those details would all be handled "off-line" by our people working together with the LDC and local bureaucrats.

Several weeks later we called the mayor and told him that the city of Rochester was quite honored by the gift of the cherry trees and wished to send the city of Yokohama 100 lilac bushes as a gesture of friendship. The mayor was elated and said he would visit our Rochester headquarters the following year and inspect the trees; he'd obviously chosen a partner that understood the importance of building friendly relations. (The cherry trees, unfortunately, were a poor match for the Rochester environs; they all succumbed to an unusually harsh winter the year they were planted.)

More than two years elapsed before we actually signed on the bottom line: we had to negotiate a lot of restrictions, such as the clause requiring us to hold the parcel for at least ten years in compliance with new land speculation laws (land speculation was in part blamed for

Japan's "bubble economy"). It wasn't until the building was completed that we actually received title to the land, and in retrospect we did take a bit of risk by going ahead with the construction. But at the same time, we really didn't have any options. In addition to needing the R&D facility to stay competitive, it would have been nearly impossible to find a parcel like the one we'd been invited to purchase, and the bureaucratic process anywhere else probably wouldn't have been much faster. Besides, land was constantly climbing in price, and the longer we waited, the higher the cost.

After finishing the lab facility, we realized that we needed more storage space and sought two more land parcels across the street. They were ours for the taking, but the price had become prohibitive: 3 million yen per *tsubo* (about $500 per square foot), making it five times as expensive as the original parcel we bought. So we opted to change our methods and use less chemical on site, possibly renting storage space in the future.

While it would have been no problem for us to rent space in the Kohoku New Town area—we'd already been deemed good corporate citizens—renting office space elsewhere was subject to the same highly competitive process as buying land. Potential candidates for space need to demonstrate why they would make a worthy tenant.

I had an opportunity to play the rental game shortly after moving into our research facility, when we were undergoing a reorganization that would necessitate moving to a larger complete office. We selected a building owned by Mori-*san*, an aging businessman whose company controlled more rental space in Tokyo than any other in the country. After submitting an application, Mori-*san*'s spokesperson called me to say that his boss would normally have come to visit us but that he was too ill to travel. I told him that I'd be extremely honored to meet with Mori-*san* at his own home office, at his convenience. A meeting was set up, and I was surprised to find the office space mogul to be dressed in formal business attire—from the previous century. In his fancy black kimono, Mori-*san* indeed looked very Japanese and very ready to play the traditional role of landlord. Apparently, he liked the fact that I'd traveled to see him; by the time I returned to my office, I found a message from his real estate company welcoming us as the new tenant.

In Japan, human relations capital is often more important than hard cash.

FILL 'ER UP!
Welcome to Service Japan

"Definitely the two-tone Leopard," Chiwata-san advised us. "It's the right car for an American executive and his wife." We looked at the picture of the automobile in the catalog and agreed that the Leopard could well be the car for the Siegs of Kodak. Chiwata-san then sent an employee to fetch the car and had tea poured for us while we waited at the showroom office. About ten minutes later, we were running our hands over the Leopard's smooth hood. Chiwata-san had a point, the car was dignified but at the same time had a touch of pizzazz with its blue top and silver gray bottom (considered much too risqué for most Japanese but perfect for gaijin). "Sold," I said, extending my hand.

Like so many shopping experiences in Japan, buying a car is associated with superb service. That means having the dealership handle all the details, like contacting the police department about the purchase and taking a local policeman or policewoman to your house to prove that you have a parking space, taking care of all the registration and license plate papers, obtaining inspection stickers, delivering the car to your door when all the paperwork is done, and even taking you out for a test drive to teach you about all the features of the car and how they work.

But wait, there's more! When the car arrives, the salesperson will likely give the owner a gift—in our case, a box of tools and cleaning supplies. Our man, Chiwata-*san*, was also quite proud of the license plate he'd picked out for us—5959 with some fancy *kanji* script. It was very elegant and appropriate for us, he explained.

Car salespeople are expected to stay with the owner for the life of the car, tracking the service record and calling when it's time for routine maintenance. Right on schedule for the checkup, Chiwata-*san* sent an employee to pick up our car. When I returned home from work the day of the maintenance check, I found the Leopard neatly parked in the garage. A week later, a bill for the service arrived.

About two years after we bought our car, Chiwata-*san* became concerned that people of our stature were driving a car that was nearly three years old. "It would be an embarrassment," he explained. "Expensive too." Chiwata-*san* was referring to the third-year mandatory inspection, which can cost hundreds of dollars to meet all of the stringent government requirements. Rather than go through such a costly ordeal, many Japanese prefer to trade in their cars and purchase a new one. That's why you'll see so few older cars on the roads in

Japan, and why you won't find many used-car dealers; the dealers sell their trade-ins to other Asian countries as well as to countries in Eastern Europe and former members of the Soviet Union.

The incentive to ditch a car before three years is bolstered by door-to-door salespeople, particularly in Japanese neighborhoods. It's not uncommon for a salesperson to ring a doorbell and say something like, "I see that your car is two-and-a-half years old. I know that you don't want to be bothered with the three-year inspection, so why not buy a new one. . . ." At which point he'll show the prospect a number of color brochures featuring various models and styles. What could be easier?

Not much, except perhaps getting the gas tank filled, as I discovered a few weeks after I'd used up the full tank of gas that Chiwata-*san* had provided. When I pulled into the station, I was greeted by a troupe of six attendants who hollered out, in unison, "*Irasshaimase!*" (Welcome). They told me where to stop the car and escorted me to the gas station office. I noticed that the uniforms were pressed and spotless and their hands showed no signs of grease. (The scene reminded me of the old "Texaco Man" commercials of the 1960s, featuring immaculately dressed attendants who treat cars with the same care and concern as a brain surgeon would give a patient undergoing a delicate operation.)

One of the attendants then filled the tank from a hose coiled up in a canopy over the filling station. (Gas stations, like everything else in Japan, are severely constrained by space, so you won't find pumps or islands; rather, the hoses are stored in retractable coils in the overhead canopies.) While the attendants filled the tank and checked all the fluids in the Leopard, I read a magazine and bought a can of coffee

from a vending machine. I looked up to see one attendant washing the windows inside and out and another running the floor mats through cleaning machines equipped with stiff brushes.

When the ablutions were complete, I was informed that my car was ready and was handed a receipt listing how many liters of gasoline I'd purchased, the price per liter, the octane, and other information about the fill-up. I paid the bill, and the attendants bowed as I got back into the car. What more could I ask for? How about an escort back into the heavy Tokyo traffic? As a normal part of the service, the attendants dashed into the oncoming stream of cars and held up their hands. Even taxi cabs stopped. As I pulled out of the station, I heard a resounding *"Arigato!"* (Thank you).

As my tenure in Japan continued, I came to notice other examples of stunning service just about everywhere. When we visited a department store, for instance, we were greeted at each floor by the elevator operators; if we were one of the first customers, we'd find the salespeople lined up by the door, bowing as we entered and calling out, in unison, *"Irasshaimase!"* When we bought our VCR, a representative from the store not only delivered the unit but hooked it up for us and tested it. He also gave us several blank tapes as a gift. Our local baker would always toss in some cookies when my wife bought bread, saying *sabisu* (service) when she looked surprised at the generosity. When we flew from Tokyo to Osaka, although the flight was only one hour, we flew in a luxurious 747. And despite the other 498 passengers on board, we were served refreshments and a snack: there was one flight attendant for about every twenty people!

I once asked my Japanese friends about the extraordinary service, and they looked surprised by my inquiry: "We pay high prices and

expect the best service," they answered. Toward the end of my stay, though, I noticed that things began slightly changing; more businesses were beginning to compete on the basis of price alone, offering what by Japanese standards are considered "bare-bone" deals—just the goods. And in today's environment, as companies compete for the shrinking supply of consumers' yen, a tremendous opportunity awaits Western businesses that don't have access to large service corps or labor pools. In the past, lower prices were associated with inferior goods; if a consumer wanted quality, he or she paid for it. Today, lower prices no longer carry that stigma, and it's not uncommon to see people walking out of Akihabara (an enormous electronic goods bazaar; see page 117) with a VCR under an arm or a TV in tote.

Even so, the concept of service is so deeply ingrained in the culture that some element of it will always play an important role in Japanese pricing and purchasing decisions. And on one level, that's good news for foreigners. Next time around I'd certainly hate to face the automotive bureaucracy on my own!

If "location, location, location" is the key to success in the United States, service, service, service is the royal road to the Japanese yen.

PIE IN THE SKY
Why the Japanese Love Information

"And what is that building?" asked one of the twelve Japanese businessmen on the minibus as the Kodak Park tour guide waited for the stoplight to turn green. "Oh that?" the guide responded. "It's now used for administrative purposes. Back in the 1960s, though, it housed the Park's bakery, the finest in all of Rochester, New York. I think it used to make 600 pies every day for all the cafeterias in the plant." At that point, the visitor sitting next to me pulled out a notebook from his coat pocket and wrote down the bakery statistics.

"Excuse me," I said, "but I couldn't help but observe that you're taking copious notes. We don't have any objections, but what in the world is so interesting about the number of pies baked twenty years ago?"

"As you know, information is a very important tool," he replied. "I'm expected by my company to return with a report

on everything I've learned. I have no idea why the information about the pies might be valuable. But it could be a very important piece of a puzzle in the future."

The more factories we visited in Japan, the more requests we received from Japanese companies to visit Kodak Park (KP), our Rochester-based manufacturing facility. Kodak Park was known throughout the world as one of the great manufacturing sites of modern times, with its 250 buildings occupying 25,000 million square feet on 12 square miles near the Genesee River. In the 1960s and 1970s nearly 45,000 people worked at KP, although downsizing in the late 1980s and early 1990s has cut that number in half.

Even with staff reductions, the Park was impressive by any standards, and, whenever possible, headquarters was delighted to respond favorably to the tour requests. In one instance, JETRO, the Japan External Trade Organization, which assembled a tour of fifteen member companies, called me to see if I would help arrange for a visit to KP. I said I'd contact corporate for them and was pleased to report back that the visit had been approved. What I didn't know was that since my next trip to Rochester for routine business would coincide with JETRO's arrival, I would be available to accompany the troupe on a full-day tour of the Park.

While I was anxious to tend to business at home and visit with Rochester friends, I did find it fun to do the all-day tour on my own turf. And the comment by the Japanese businessman about the pies actually helped me frame an understanding of the role of informa-

tion in Japan. On the one hand, the odds are probably a hundred trillion to one that the daily number of pies made twenty years ago at a now-defunct bakery in Kodak Park could possibly be "a very important piece of a puzzle in the future." But on the other hand, it represents a willingness to keep an open mind and soak up everything about one's immediate environment. As a result of their propensity to absorb information, the Japanese are probably the most factually knowledgeable people on the planet. While the simple knowledge of facts doesn't guarantee brilliant decision making, it still provides an incredibly useful base for solving problems and charting a course into the future.

Thinking in terms of "total information" also gives the Japanese a leg up during negotiations with Westerners. I'd often found myself at a psychological disadvantage when the negotiator on the other side of the table knew so much about me and my family: it was almost like talking with my mother. When we were setting up our Japanese operations, for example, I visited several banks and was stunned to discover that they knew where I went to school, my degree, the names of my family members, what I like to do for leisure activities, and various positions I'd held at Kodak. Now, most of this was public information and could be obtained with a little bit of digging. But it was nevertheless unnerving that the bankers already had memorized my resume.

As in the case of the pies, much of what the bank had learned was irrelevant on a practical scale. But from a negotiating standpoint, it was indeed a "very important piece" of a larger puzzle. That's because the Japanese don't negotiate on the basis of one company or organization; rather, they maneuver on the basis of relationships. So if the

people on the "other side" knew I hated fishing but loved golf, they'd be sure to avoid talk about fishing and focus heavily on golf during the "warm-up" phase of the negotiation. It seems like a simplistic ploy, but it really can stack the deck in their favor.

Some say the craving to "know everything" originates with a classical Japanese text, *The Five Rings*, penned by the famous Samurai Musashi in the 1600s after he retired and went into seclusion. In his book, Musashi outlined five attributes of a military strategy for overcoming an opponent who was stronger than you are. One of the strategies discusses information as the underpinning of any successful competitive effort and exhorts the reader to learn everything that can possibly be learned about the enemy.

More recently, the renowned scholar Ikujiro Nonaka, who teaches at Hitotsubashi University in what amounts to the Japanese equivalent of an M.B.A. program, commented at a seminar, "In an economy where the only certainty is uncertainty, the one sure source of lasting competitive advantage is knowledge. And knowledge is power. It is not a pious truism. It is a basic operating principle."

The Japanese prepare the next generation to deal with uncertainty by teaching them to cherish the acquisition of raw information at a very early age. As children progress through their school years, they learn the art of memorizing vast quantities of facts. Teachers often recite from textbooks, while students take copious notes so they can spew it back on tests. Even science and math are taught purely on the basis of memorization.

When students reach the high school level, the memorization becomes more intense. And if you ask high school students why there's such a strong emphasis on the accumulation of facts in their

culture, they'll often remind you about the unique demands of their language: in order to graduate, people need to know how to read and write 2,000 characters, and there's no way to do that except by brute memory.

That early emphasis on memory during all phases of schooling tends to cultivate an insatiable thirst for information and a strong tendency, especially among businesspeople, to sop up every factoid they encounter. Regardless of what percentage of the facts might be "very important pieces" in search of "big puzzles," the *ability* to ferret out information can pay off handsomely, especially in the area of competitor intelligence. As one of our marketing experts, an English-man named Bill Hall, put it, "If you look at the British approach to gathering competitor information, it's, 'Well, what we mean, chaps, is that we read the chairman of the board's statement in the annual report, we check the newspaper clippings, then somehow or other we divine what the competitors are doing.' The American approach is, 'We talk to our securities analyst.' And the Japanese approach is, 'We count the number of trucks that leave a competitor's warehouse per hour, find out how many of the trucks are owned and how many are leased, then learn their pricing structures by interviewing their whole-salers or distributors.' "

While Hall's observation is a bit tongue in cheek, it does contain a lot of truth: Japanese companies can relentlessly attack and counter-attack in any marketplace because of their superb competitor intel-ligence. They've also learned how to leverage their accumulation of information by collaborating on the innovation end of new products and then competing on the distribution and marketing. This competi-tive energy is the fuel that drives the Japanese economic engine.

Amused as we might have been about the Japanese attitude about acquiring facts, Kodak Japan would have been much better off if it had taken competitor information gathering more seriously. We originally set up our office in Japan to figure out how we could better meet our customer needs, not tangle with competitors. But in retrospect, without good competitor research, we were always in a reactive mode, responding to each wave of attack and counterattack as it rolled through the marketplace.

I still think that the defunct bakery statistic has a hundred-trillion-to-one chance to be useful. But a little pie-in-the-sky thinking about information might not be such a bad thing after all.

Never underestimate the power of "infomania," even if 95 percent is superfluous, the remaining 5 percent can be a powerful competitive weapon.

Mount Fuji from the window of a JAL 747.

New Year Festival Time at the entrance to the Asakusa Kannon Temple in northern Tokyo.

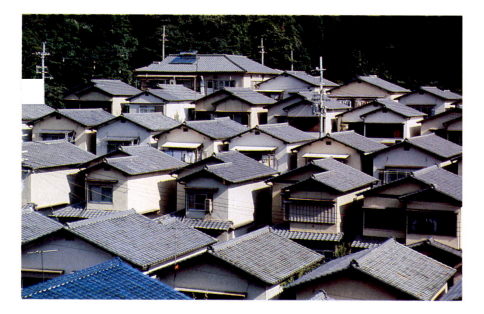

Suburban Tokyo.

Kodak's High Profile Sign in Ginza... After waiting four years for the building to be completed and receiving the mandatory blessing from a Shinto priest, we finally had our sign. Fuji film had an equally large sign erected across the street in a matter of months.

The Kodak Go airship flying over downtown Tokyo. The corporate offices of Fuji were one of our favorite airborne destinations.

Infomania… The Japanese have more magazines, many of them weeklies, than any other nation in the world.

Akihabara... The main corner of the world's largest shopping district for electronic equipment and appliances.

Political protest march in Tokyo demonstrating against changes in the Japanese educational system.

An Osaka morning.

Tokyo Bay from my office window.

Pre-schoolers on a temple visit. This group of children were part of an elite prep school, the first step in ensuring that each child attended all of the "number one" schools.

The Shinjinrui, "The New People" in Yoyoyogi Park in downtown Tokyo. Teens travel to the park every Sunday in their school uniforms and then change their hair and clothes and party to rock bands.

Gurupu—*Japanese Style*—*The carrying of the Mikoshi is a ritual honoring the local deity. Weighing several tons, it takes precise teamwork to move the* Mikoshi *through teeming crowds to its final destination.*

Several dozen of the 1,000 Torii *gates at the shrine of Fushimi Inari, built to honor agriculture and business. Each* Torii *gate was donated to the temple by a group or individual who had experienced some good fortune in their business enterprise.*

Japanese dining in a downtown Osaka restaurant. Each of the red lanterns displays an item available on the menu.

The future Japanese consumer in Azabu Juban, one of the oldest shopping districts in Tokyo.

Wendy's—Japanese Style... The Azabu Juban section of Tokyo has more Mercedes Benzs per square mile than anywhere in Germany.

There's always a Colonel out front at Kentucky Fried Chicken in Hiroo.

Rice Farming in the Karuizawa area, the foothills of the Japanese Alps.

Osaka Castle—built in 1586. This reproduction of the original castle was built in 1931. This was once the mightiest fortress in Japan.

Sumo wrestling, the national pastime, in the Kikan in Tokyo.

A traditional Kabuki actor preparing for his performance.

The Japanese "Bullet Train" or Shinkansen (*the new train*), *pulling into the station.*

National elections in Tokyo... All electioneering takes place over a several week period. Unlike the U.S., most campaigning takes the form of billboards, like this one, and street rallies.

The Pagoda at the Kiyomizu Temple in Kyoto. Built in 1633 and surrounded by cherry trees, it represents the importance of tradition and beauty in Japanese life.

MOLDING PUTTY
Training Your New Japanese Employees

The fall of 1987 was an exciting time at Kodak Japan; for the first time, we were going to recruit college grads. Our head of human relations, Mihashi-san, presented his step-by-step plan for contacting professors, visiting campuses with literature, writing a recruitment brochure, and so on. I nodded with approval as I read through the plan and then did a double-take when I read the last line: "Training program: Six months."

"Must be a typo," I suggested to Mihashi-san. "Did you mean six days?"

"Oh no, Sieg-san," he replied. "We'll need six months to train the new employees."

"But the recruits are going to be salespeople and marketing people and administrative assistants. Explain to me why we

don't just give them a two-day orientation and send 'em on the road or to their offices."

"Because they're just college grads. How could they possibly be ready for work yet?"

In Japan, college grads trained in nontechnical areas arrive on a company's doorstep with a vast amount of memorized material in their heads and a lot of determination. You know that they'll try their very hardest, having been inculcated with the *gambatte* mentality from early in life. Or as Mary White of Harvard University summed up the Japanese experience of elementary schooling, "In the lower grades, one should learn to bear hardship, and in the middle grades to persist to the end with patience, and in the upper grades, to be steadfast and accomplish goals undaunted by obstacles or failure." To that, I would add that college is an unusual time between high school and work largely devoted to developing the networks on which students will depend in the future.

With that as a backdrop, all a company has to do is shape the grads into problem solvers and productive workers. The process, as explained to me, is like molding "putty" for the workplace. And that's exactly how the Japanese industrial complex wants it, conveying to the Ministry of Education that it seeks "raw material" imbued with strong virtues and qualities, but still malleable enough to be trained to mesh with the company.

All this was very strange to me, since in the United States we think of the labor market in terms of matching jobs and skills, not people and companies, as it is conceived of in Japan. Put another way, we're

used to hiring college grads, or anyone else, for specific job positions, rather than recruiting a group of people to be deployed once you figure out where they can fit into the organization. The situation for grads trained in the sciences and technical areas was somewhat more like that in the West, as they arrived with training in specific disciplines and could start off in their labs or divisions with less "shaping." But those schooled in a general college curriculum could wind up anywhere in the company—from sales to operations—following the intensive in-house training.

Since I had no experience with these employee hiring and training techniques, I decided to take an observer's role to see how it's done, following the lead of our human relations staff. Actually, I wasn't totally passive; we began the training of the "class of '88" with a major entrance ceremony at which, as president, I was expected to offer a twenty-minute welcoming address in Japanese. I actually made the speech in English, but we passed out a written translation in Japanese. While my speech didn't say anything about lifetime employment, it did stress that even though we were a foreign capital company, we were making a long-term investment in Japan and our people and hoped that they would be with us for a very long time. Our human relations staff then suggested that two or three of the trainees respond from their point of view. They talked about their good fortune at being selected by such a well-known, world-class company.

After the ceremony, the thirty trainees (who soon developed tight social bonds by virtue of the tremendous amounts of time they spent together) began their indoctrination into the company, starting with a review of the company structure, the different departments, the names of the department heads, the multiple sites and what happens at each

location, and so on. The trainees had to study the information carefully because they'd be quizzed on all the details.

Next, the general affairs people came in and discussed the company's performance over the last couple of years, the general terms of the company's plans for the coming year, and the goals for achieving market share. In our case, since we were a foreign capital company, our recruits learned about Eastman Kodak's activities worldwide—its various manufacturing locations, and R&D sites (I was drafted to relay some of the nitty-gritty information about Kodak's global activities). And since Kodak is fundamentally an imaging company, we spent three or four days during the first month giving our trainees a feel for photography by teaching them to process their own pictures.

After four weeks of orientation, the human relations staff asked our trainees to write a brief report on their personal vision for being in the company and where they thought they'd be able to contribute the most. Based on the reports, human relations people and general affairs people would assign each trainee to a department—not for actual full-time work but for on-the-job training under the wing of a mentor. The new grad was referred to as a *kobun* (new child), and the person doing the mentoring as an *oyabun* (father). After the *kobun* read documentation about departmental policies and procedures (which took about two weeks), the *oyabun* gave them very small assignments. During the next five months, the *oyabun* would carefully increase the responsibility of the assignments they doled out, until the *kobun* were ready to become full-fledged employees.

In the short term, the lengthy process is frustrating to a Westerner and very expensive if you count "widgets per employee," as we do in the United States. But Japanese firms expect to retain employees for

the long haul, so they feel it's well worth the heavy investment in internal training.

About 10 to 15 percent of the Japanese workforce is mobile and willing to make midcareer changes, and most of these people start off working in small companies of 100 or less or in *gaishi* or foreign companies. Once Japanese employees make the switch in mentality, they're willing to move from company to company. But most employers are fairly safe in their assumption that internal training is worth the cost.

All of this focus on training and maintaining a satisfied workforce elevates the position of the human relations director to an extremely important level. In fact, many Japanese presidents occupy the HR director slot just before assuming their role as head of the company. By contrast, in the United States, human resources isn't generally regarded as a pathway to the corner office. That fact alone pretty well sums up the differences between our view and the Japanese view of just what people are really worth in the business equation.

Don't expect new Japanese college grads to raise the productivity of your company today; invest in their future and they'll help create yours.

I'VE COME TO EXPLAIN WHY I CAN'T ACCEPT YOUR JOB OFFER

Hiring Japanese to Work in a Gaijin Company

When my secretary, Hioki-san, told me that Kawamoto-san
was waiting in the conference room, I was certain that I'd
finally convinced the talented young engineer to come work for
us at Kodak. After courting him for more than a year, I
thought to myself that all the time and effort had been worth it:
Kawamoto-san would be a great asset to our product-
development program. Upon arriving at the conference room, I
encountered Kawamoto-san's close family: his wife, father, and
mother. Perhaps it was in the Japanese tradition to trot
everyone out when making a momentous career announcement.

One of the first things my Japanese colleagues warned me about was the difficulty Western companies experience in attracting top Japanese college graduates. Most of the grads want to work for the government bureaucracy or the most prestigious Japanese companies, since both career paths offer the promise of lifetime employment (although in the 1990s the employment-for-life concept began to bend under the weight of a sagging economy). And just as Japanese students want to work for top organizations, Japanese companies compete fiercely for grads from the top four or five universities.

Tokyo University (*Todai*, short for *Tokyo Daigaku*—the Japanese have a great penchant for contractions) sits at the top of the prestige list. *Todai* grads can write their own tickets, although few of them choose to work for non-Japanese companies. In my seven years in Japan, Kodak was able to lure only one *Todai* graduate to join us, and that happened after many months of courting the fellow's professor. The reason for this seemingly indirect route is that professors hold a great deal of power in the employment process, since they're expected to place their best students in the "right" companies. So in order for a company to gain an "allocation" from a particular professor, it must develop a long-term relationship with him and demonstrate that it is worthy of receiving his students. The flip side of all this is that if you don't hire a professor's student once he's made a placement recommendation, you'll never see another recommendation from his department.

To begin building a relationship with a professor, endow a chair at his university, or establish a series of merit scholarships and summer internships. The latter approach is particularly effective with technical students, who are the most in demand and therefore the most difficult to attract.

After developing a relationship with a professor and establishing a track record as a good employer that has made a long-term commitment to Japan, it gets easier to lure grads from the better universities. The "stigma" of being a *gaijin* company, however, will always be a barrier. Kodak once negotiated an agreement to hire a person from the government agency MITI (Ministry of International Trade and Industry). The most difficult part was convincing the person's supervisor that we wouldn't destroy his protégé's career with an ill-timed move to a foreign capital company.

Why all this effort to recruit graduates from a particular school? In Japan, hiring someone means far more than just bringing an employee on board: it's tantamount to acquiring an entire *network* of important connections—the student's classmates. The better the school, the better the companies that the students will be working for, and therefore, the more valuable their peer networks. Some of the grads will go to work for the government, which makes their connections extremely valuable. These people provide a tremendous amount of knowledge and inside information about navigating through the bureaucracy.

Now, it's important to keep in mind that the choice of students and their networks has nothing to do with brainpower; perfectly qualified and highly intelligent people may attend a "lesser" university because they didn't have the resources to get into the best primary and secondary schools that in turn feed the most elite universities. So the students who graduate from the lower-tier universities may well be just as smart or even smarter than their counterparts in the *Todai* league, but their networks won't be of the same quality.

I witnessed first-hand the power of peer networks early in my tenure at Kodak Japan when one of our research labs was developing a new type of document scanner and needed a very special electronic component that wasn't commercially available at the time. An R&D engineer in our lab knew someone—an old classmate—in another company that would be marketing the component in the future. A single phone call in the morning was all it took for the rare part to materialize on our lab bench in the afternoon! Had we gone through normal channels, our team would have been simply told that the component wasn't being sold yet—try again in six months.

That experience made me quite open to currying the favor of Japanese professors in subject areas that were of importance to us, and Kodak began planning for an endowment. Since this could take several years for the effort to pay off, I tried a shortcut—the "internal recommendation" method. We asked our Japanese engineers to see if they had any friends who might be interested in working for us, and one actually gave me the name of a potential candidate, Kawamoto-*san*, an engineer who seemed perfect for our electronic device development area. Kawamoto-*san*'s credentials were excellent, and since Kodak was trying to build up its electronic product division, we wanted to discuss with him the possibility of his becoming one of four or five key supervisors.

Kawamoto-*san* was rather surprised when we called for a job interview, and I sensed a tinge of guilt when he finally agreed to come by the lab. To be sure, he was quite impressed by the resources and equipment, and while he didn't show it outwardly, I think he found the "freewheeling" style of the company very attractive. After a two-hour tour and chat, I made the job offer, and Kawamoto-*san* said that he would get back to us very soon with a decision.

A month passed with no response, so I assumed that Kawamoto-*san* had declined our offer. But a month after that, he called to ask if he could come and visit us again. I figured that he'd want to discuss fine points of the job offer, but when he arrived, he simply asked the same kinds of general questions he'd asked the first time around, and no new ground was broken. Kawamoto-*san* again said that he'd be in touch, and another month elapsed, during which time the friend who recommended him assured me that Kawamoto-*san* was still interested; he just had to think about leaving a very prestigious firm for foreign money. There was family pressure, too, my engineer explained.

The pattern of interviews and silence continued for many months, and my colleagues and I were growing annoyed with the situation. So I was most curious when I found Kawamoto-*san* and his familial entourage standing in our conference room. Normally, I would have invited everyone to sit down in the plush, low-back chairs arranged around a low coffee table. (Japanese conference rooms don't sport gargantuan tables like those found in typical U.S. companies. Rather than being designed for presentations and negotiations, the Japanese arrangement is geared for easy chat about a golf game and then pleasant talk about the business at hand.) But before I could offer the amenities of chairs and tea, Kawamoto-*san*'s father bowed and said, "Sieg-*san*, I'm sorry to say that my son cannot accept your offer to work at Kodak. Our family is very concerned about our son's future and have met to discuss the situation. Unfortunately, we cannot come to an understanding about Kawamoto-*san*'s desire's to work for Eastman Kodak. So after much discussion, we have all agreed that our son should not leave his current position." The father then profusely apologized for the trouble and discomfort

I'VE COME TO EXPLAIN WHY I CAN'T ACCEPT YOUR OFFER

his son had caused our firm, after which he led the troupe out the door in single file.

Ironically, a month after Kawamoto-*san* declined our job offer, Eastman Kodak acquired the company in which Kawamoto-*san* worked. We didn't get the network, but we did, in a sense, get our man!

Build trust in the academic community, government circles, and the population at large, and top Japanese talent will follow.

I GIVE YOU
MY FEELINGS
On the Role of Money in Japan

Hioki-san, my secretary, could hardly contain herself when she walked into my office waving a fancy-looking envelope. "Look what you got, Sieg-san!" she said.

"What is it?" I asked, trying to read the kanji.

"A wedding invitation from Kimura-san [president of a subsidiary company whose son, the groom, had just joined Kodak Japan as an entry-level employee]."

Later that day, I ran through a list of possible gifts for the bride and groom—a fancy serving bowl, some silverware, a toaster. "No, Sieg-san," Aki said with a laugh, "when you go to a Japanese wedding you give money. And then the newlyweds will give you a gift in return. By the way, Sieg-san, as the head of the company where Kimura-san works, you'll be expected to make a speech in Japanese. We'd better start practicing very soon."

Make a speech! It was bad enough that I had to sing in public at *karaoke* bars and play golf, two things that have about the same appeal to me as a case of rabies. But making a speech in Japanese. . . . Really.

At least the money part will be easy, I thought to myself. Just put a check in a card and send it to the bride and groom. Wrong again. In Japan, money plays many unique social roles, and the giving of money is shrouded in all kinds of rituals. When the Japanese hand money to each other they usually say, "*Kimochi desu*" (These are my feelings that I'm giving you). The words *kimochi desu* cast a magical spell, transforming the cash into a kind of social currency. Or as Kase-*san*, an advisor to former prime minister Nakasone, once explained during a seminar, verbal communication is not as well developed in Japan as it is in Western cultures, so that key expressions tend to impart far more than their literal meaning. The passing of money, when accompanied by *kimochi desu*, becomes a symbolic offering, and the cash itself becomes a kind of lubricant that maintains harmonious interactions in the Japanese social structure.

Given the symbolic nature and social functions of money, it's acceptable, even expected, to give cash gifts for all sorts of occasions—a wedding, a birth, a death, or graduations, as well as for the many official holidays that the Japanese observe. The recipient of a gift then reciprocates and gives the giver a gift valued at 25 to 50 percent of the cash amount. The government recognizes the strain that this might place on newlyweds, though, and allows them to deduct the amount of the *keicho-hi* (return gifts) from the cash gifts that they received at the wedding (the Japanese pay taxes on cash gifts).

Other than specific occasions and holidays, Japan observes two independent gift-giving seasons: one at the beginning of the year, the

other at midyear. During the independent seasons, it's acceptable to give people noncash presents, such as rice crackers or whisky. Seaweed, however, is considered the top gift and reflects the deepest feelings. (You can always tell when gift season is approaching by the frenetic activity around the receiving areas of department stores as they stock up for heavy-duty foot traffic and sales.)

Gift season aside, cash gifts are the universal way of "connecting" in Japan. And given the symbolic nature and social function of money, money is often passed along in ways that would be frowned upon in the West. For instance, it's perfectly acceptable for local political figures to give money to newlyweds in their districts or for businesses to give cash gifts to diet members or other government officials. Only when extraordinary sums of money are involved does the gift cross the line from a normal social practice to influence peddling, as in the Recruit scandal involving millions of dollars in payoffs to politicians in exchange for government business.

To avoid any implications of impropriety, Kodak had a cast-in-stone policy of not giving cash gifts of any size to political or government figures—despite protests from our Japanese top managers who felt that we were missing an opportunity to fit into the culture and "grease" the bureaucratic machinery. In retrospect, we may have been too cautious, and we should have played the money game; had we done so, we probably would have been able to maneuver more quickly through the bureaucracy during our critical start-up period. And we could have done so without compromising our integrity, too, since the practice has been normalized throughout all strata of Japanese society.

Eventually, Kodak Japan did get into the annual gift seasons, and we offered presents to our most significant customers or suppliers.

I grudgingly learned to accept gifts that seemed appropriate too. One of our larger customers once gave me four "box seat" tickets to a sumo wrestling match, and my Japanese colleagues, fearful that I would make a major social faux pas that would permanently damage our relationship with the customer, convinced me to use the tickets. So Irma and I, along with another American couple, rode the subway to the arena, took off our shoes, and were led to the "box"—actually, a rice mat about one meter square. Before the event, we were brought four large shopping bags full of snacks, sake, and gifts. We tipped the people who seated us and brought the gifts, passing along the money with a sincere *kimochi desu*. (About midway through, one of my guests, a large-framed fellow who weighed in at 230 pounds, could no longer stand the cramps in his thighs and wound up wrapping his aching legs around the three of us. This strange *gaijin* scene brought us almost as much attention as the wrestlers!)

Several weeks after the sumo match, it was time to prepare for the wedding. Once again, Hioki-*san* saved the day for me, this time by helping to determine how much money I should give to the bride and groom. The situation was complicated by the fact that other people from our office were invited to attend the event, and it would be inappropriate if any of them gave more cash than I did. Therefore, I had to give a large enough gift so that no one would inadvertently outdo me. We decided that 100,000 yen ($600 at the time) would leave enough room for each tier of the company to offer a decreasing amount. I would count on Hioki-*san* to leak out the information so that it filtered through the ranks.

Hioki-*san* then did some shopping for me, stopping first at the bank for brand new bills; it would have been considered very poor

taste to give anything slightly rumpled. She then stopped at a local stationery store to pick out an appropriate envelope for the couple-to-be (an entire paper industry has evolved around paraphernalia for passing along gift money), as well as a gold string with tassels and a *furoshiki* (a scarf-like piece of cloth for wrapping the envelope). Aki wrote an appropriate note on the envelope, then wrapped it in the *furoshiki* according to custom. Now I was all set to carry the gift to the wedding, unwrap the *furoshiki*, and place the envelope in the receiving box. No one would know that a *gaijin* had anything to do with the preparation of this gift!

Finally, there was the matter of the speech, which Aki advised me should begin with the well-wishing phrase *Omedeto gozaimasu* (Congratulations on getting married). Next, I was to speak very briefly about the groom. Since I'd met him only once, and just for a few minutes at that, it was easy to be brief. Then I was to talk about the groom's father, particularly how important he was to the Eastman Kodak company and the terrific contributions he'd made over the years. I was to close with a standard line, *Kokoro kara no oiwai o itadakimasu* (From my heart, my congratulations). I must have repeated the speech thirty times in the week preceding the wedding, and with the patience of a saint, Aki corrected my pronunciation after each recitation.

The wedding was delightful and I'm told that the speech went well. "I could understand each word, Sieg-*san*," one of my Japanese colleagues said the next day when we were back at the office. That's a tribute to Aki's tutelage and patience more than anything else.

A month after the wedding, a box arrived at the office via a "black cat" express truck (the Japanese equivalent of UPS. The trucks are

bright yellow and with a caricature of a black cat on them). "Oh great, just what I need—another obligation," I said to myself, figuring that it must be a gift from a vendor. But Aki picked up the card, and seeing the look of puzzlement on my face, explained that it was a return gift from Kimura-*san*. "A nice gesture," I said to her. "Does that mean I have to send another gift?" She shook her head indicating that I was in the clear, then walked back to her desk.

In Japanese business and social life, meeting obligations is of paramount importance; money wipes the slate clean.

AN APOLOGY TO THE MAN IN OSAKA
Maintaining Harmony in Japanese Society

"A 'three-shower' day!" Sawada-san said to me with a smile as he watched me wipe the sweat from my brow with a handkerchief. It was bad enough that we were wearing dark-colored business suits in the midst of an intense heat wave—90 degree temperatures and 90 percent humidity—while traveling four hours by train and another hour by (unairconditioned) taxicab. To add insult to injury, all of this was to apologize to one angry customer!

The customer's problem actually began in 1976, when Eastman Kodak announced that it planned to offer a line of instant cameras. Within days of the announcement, Polaroid filed a lawsuit claiming that Kodak had violated a number of its patents. Many years later, Polaroid triumphed in court and Kodak was required to pay a staggering multimillion-dollar fine. In addition, the judge handed Kodak a cease-and-desist order, which meant that Kodak would not only have to stop manufacturing instant cameras, but that it would have to recall and destroy all the cameras that it had already sold.

To comply with the order, Kodak initiated a return program: customers could turn in their instant cameras and receive brand new, equivalently valued Kodak 35 millimeter cameras in exchange. While this went over well in the United States, some Japanese consumers weren't overjoyed by the prospect of owning a Kodak 35 mm camera: high-quality 35 mm cameras were available everywhere in Japan and at bargain prices, too. So in Japan we also began a cash buyback program for owners of Kodak instant cameras, paying what we determined was a fair price per unit.

No amount of money, however, seemed adequate to Sugisaki-*san*, an Osaka resident who took his outrage to the local press and eventually managed to snag the interest of the national media. (The Japanese press loves to run stories about the untrustworthy nature of foreign companies, so this act of business "treachery" made for great copy.)

At first I took the American approach to the problem, telling my people simply to ignore Sugisaki-*san*. "He'll get tired of this and go away," I said confidently. But as my colleagues predicted, Sugisaki-*san* relentlessly hammered away at Kodak, and some in my office feared that his campaign could eventually prove to be a major embarrassment for us. Nothing—letters, phone calls, and visits from our

staff—placated this one-man PR disaster force. Finally, Sawada-*san*, one of our Japanese subsidiary presidents, informed me that the only way to end the matter was to pay Sugisaki-*san* a visit and offer him an *owabi*—an apology. Apparently the full-page ads explaining Kodak's situation and offering extensive apologies to consumers and dealers weren't enough: Sugisaki-*san* wanted to receive his apology in person.

As many foreigners quickly discover, apologies are not only a critical component of Japanese culture but are an important means of maintaining social harmony and navigating through difficult social situations. To successfully live and work among the Japanese, it's therefore necessary to be able to humble yourself and express apologies for all sorts of things. And while it's assumed that people don't inconvenience each other or commit social transgressions on purpose, "unfortunate" incidents are inevitable. And the only way to wipe the slate clean is to apologize.

Apologies clear most blame, whatever your position in life—a belief that often gets Japanese into hot water when dealing with foreigners. (Remember ex-prime minister Nakasone's attempts to backpedal and apologize for his comments about "lazy Americans" and American productivity being hampered by black workers? These comments were less gaffes than reflections of a fundamental lack of understanding that the rest of the world doesn't operate on the apology system. They also reflect the fact that Japanese leaders were not used to the international media broadcasting their words on a worldwide network. In many ways, the Japanese felt more comfortable expressing their feelings before their economic miracle brought them into the focus of the international press.)

Just as there are different ways of addressing subordinates and superiors, there are many ways of apologizing to people, depending on the situation and who's involved in it. If you're apologizing to a subordinate, you'll be more brusque than when you're apologizing to a peer. When apologizing to a superior, you'll be even more, well, "apologetic."

I had my first taste of the "apology system" soon after my wife and I arrived in Japan. Since parking was virtually impossible in the downtown area, when we went into town we'd leave the car near the train station closest to our house—a practice that our foreign friends assured us was quite legal. Following one of our downtown excursions, though, we returned to find the car missing. I walked to the nearest police box, and an officer, who understood a little bit of English, tried to help. After much arm flapping and gesturing, we were finally communicating on a common wavelength, and he pointed out the writing in chalk on the street where our car had been parked, indicating that the car had been towed. He also pointed to the no-parking sign, which, of course, I couldn't read.

Realizing that this was going to be too involved for simple sign and body language, I called my office and spoke with my secretary, Hioki-*san*, who was fluent in English. She then made several calls and learned the location where our car had been towed. We made our way to the Roppongi police station by subway, as Hioki-*san* instructed, and through an interpreter learned that we'd have to pay a fine of 5,000 yen (about $25 at the time), as well as a towing fee (almost twice the fine). In addition, I learned, we'd committed a notable offense that would be recorded on my driver's license. Nine more points and I'd be sent to the equivalent of remedial driver's ed.

This was all beginning to sound like serious stuff, but as the interpreter at the police station explained, I had a way out. The fine and the points on my license would be forgiven if I would submit a written apology explaining that my wife and I were foreigners and ignorant of the parking laws, and that we were deeply sorry for all the extra work that our ignorance had caused everyone. A police officer handed me a piece of letterhead stationery, and I set to work writing up our descent into the dark world of parking crime and humbling ourselves for violating the municipal traffic laws.

I bumped into the apology system again about a year later when I failed to comply with the alien registration laws, which require all *gaijin* to report to the local ward office or *ku* within ten days of any changes in their status; failure to do so can land them in very hot water. (*Gaijin* must also register with their ward office once per year to indicate where they live and work and how long they intend to stay and to demonstrate that they have a valid passport and visa. After being fingerprinted, they're given a new alien registration certificate, which must be carried on the body at all times. I never did find out what you're supposed to do when wearing swimming trunks.)

The status change in question involved my office telephone number, which had been switched as a matter of routine business. When I visited the ward office to report the change, I was led to a chair in front of the desk of a very polite, but officious, young woman who interrogated me for some time as to why I was so late in reporting a very important piece of information. I explained that the telephone company changed the number, and it had simply slipped my mind that I was supposed to report such events to the ward office. The young woman nodded in an approving sort of way, then handed me a form letter of apology addressed to the immigration officers. The letter stated that I was aware I had not reported change in status information within the prescribed time limits set forth by law; that I knew the consequences of my actions; that I had caused the office extra work; that I promised to pay attention to such details in the future; and, most important, that I was sorry and promised to be a better foreigner in the coming years. The letter was placed in my file in the ward office, and the incident was all but forgotten. Such is the power of apology!

Gaijin aren't the only ones expected to offer apologies. Even leaders of powerful Japanese companies have to apologize now and then. That's because heads of Japanese companies are responsible and accountable for everything (even though some say they're not really in charge of anything). The CEO or president is therefore expected to handle major apologies made on behalf of the organization; the assumption is that if the CEO or president had been doing the job properly, the problem requiring an apology never would have occurred.

This line of thinking even applies to events clearly beyond the CEO's or president's control, as in the case of the 1985 Japan Airlines tragedy in which 535 people were killed when a JAL jumbo jet slammed into a mountain. After months of inquiry, the cause of the accident was traced to a faulty bulkhead repair. Yet the president of JAL assumed responsibility for the incident and personally visited each of the victims' families to offer his humble and personal apology. He then resigned, as custom would expect him to do.

While I wasn't about to resign my position as Kodak Japan's president because of the company's involuntary withdrawal from the

instant photography market, I was certainly willing to make a trip to visit a disgruntled customer who felt he'd been terribly wronged by the turn of events in the U.S. courts—even if it required spending eight hours traveling to the outskirts of Osaka with two other top executives and a translator during a three-shower day.

When we finally arrived at Sugisaki-*san*'s house (we had to walk the last three blocks because the taxi driver couldn't find the address), I noted that it was located in a typical Japanese neighborhood—a mishmash of small and large buildings, some with "mom and pop" stores in the ground floors. The house itself was typically Japanese, measuring about ten by ten meters and constructed of stucco.

Inside, the living room was a bit unusual, as the walls were covered floor to ceiling with shelves of overflowing books, magazines, and newspapers. The room resembled a well-browsed used-bookstore, save for a *shoji* screen (a wooden frame covered with oiled paper) that separated us from a small kitchen. Sugisaki-*san*'s wife, who had greeted us at the door, disappeared behind the screen shortly after our arrival to make tea. As a show of hospitality, Sugisaki-*san* had constructed a "chair" for me out of a wooden box and a pillow; I guess he figured that I'd be uncomfortable sitting on the floor with everyone else.

After we exchanged a few pleasantries and sipped some green tea, Sugisaki-*san*, a large man in his sixties with thinning gray hair, began explaining how distressed he was about having to relinquish his instant camera. He also implied that the cash we were offering for his camera was insufficient and that he wanted the amount he originally paid for the product, which was substantially more.

Sawada-*san* listened intensely, according to Sugisaki-*san* the revered treatment that people over sixty are accustomed to receiving,

AN APOLOGY TO THE MAN IN OSAKA

then gently explained that the offer was the best Kodak could make. It was then my turn to step up to the plate and, through a translator, offer Sugisaki-*san* my own explanation of the situation. I described the facts of the lawsuit and Kodak's position, and how a great many Japanese customers were quite pleased with the offer. I also deeply apologized for the personal grief that the situation had caused him.

An hour and a half after we sat down, Sugisaki-*san* was ready to let the matter go and graciously agreed to hand me his instant camera. Too bad the camera wasn't loaded. It would have been nice to snap a group photo before we headed back for our long, sweaty ride home.

A simple apology for a business of social impropriety can buy more good will than a full-court public relations campaign.

THE TOKYO CHRONICLES
140

"WE'LL DISCUSS THIS AND GET BACK TO YOU SOON"

Negotiating an Acquisition in Japan

Kay Whitmore, president of the worldwide Eastman Kodak Company, glanced over at me and nodded his head, signaling that it was time to spell out the agenda for the rest of our meeting with the senior officials of Nagase Sangyo and Kusuda Company, our two film distributors. I took in a deep breath and steeled myself for the startling news I was about to give our guests. Shozo Nagase and Teruo Kusuda no doubt realized that the two-day meeting at the lavish Hawaiian resort was very important; otherwise, they wouldn't be sitting across the table from the president of Eastman Kodak worldwide and his top vice president, as well as Kodak Japan's most senior officials. They probably believed that we were *going to ask them to do more for Kodak in the years to come and to suggest ways to strengthen our already fine relationships with them. When I announced that we'd called the meeting to explain our plans for terminating our distribution agreement and acquiring the divisions that handled our products, our Japanese guests looked as if they'd just been informed that a student chef was preparing their puffa fish.*

Kodak had been selling photographic film in Japan for many years through a large network of distributors. In the early fifties, however, the Japanese government limited the number of distributors Kodak could use to two, in order to better control import procedures. In the official parlance of the Japanese bureaucracy, the action was taken to "end confusion" in the importing business. The companies we abandoned became the main distributors for Fuji Photo Film, so in effect we'd taught the distribution company that was to become our main competitor how to move film throughout the country's retail stores. Those distributors never forgave us, even after the government eased restrictions and we attempted to expand our network; many told us in no uncertain terms that they would never work with us because of the way we treated them in the past. Instead, they stuck with Fuji and became part of one of Japan's most successful alliances.

In the early 1980s, top management in Rochester felt that Kodak had gone about as far as it could in Japan without actually having a base of operations there. Moreover, Fuji had made remarkable leaps in product quality and suddenly found itself capable of making deep

inroads into the U.S. and European marketplaces. So it seemed appropriate that we should fight fire with fire and try to enhance our penetration of the Japanese market. To do so, however, we would have to study the situation first hand; there's only so much you can do when separated from the marketplace by a very large ocean.

I was selected to lead a team to Tokyo to assess Kodak's future growth and business potential in Japan and to develop a strategy, if possible, for enhancing our position there. Within six months it became clear that to succeed in Japan, we'd have to take control of our own distribution; the third-party distributors weren't aligned strategically with our company. We could do this by building a distribution network from scratch or buying the existing one from Nagase Sangyo and Kusuda. The former approach would have been difficult and slow; we didn't have the people, organizations, or relationships with retailers to move our product into the hands of consumers. The latter approach would require extraordinary acts of delicacy and diplomacy but really didn't have a downside if we negotiated a deal that pleased everyone.

So our best choice was to go the acquisition route and hope that the negotiations would not become too onerous or time consuming. In the case of Kusuda, the matter was relatively simple; we would simply propose to buy the photographic division of the company. Nagase's situation was far more complex. The several-hundred-million-dollar trading company's Division for Kodak Products, as it was called, involved more than 1,000 people who would, through no will of their own, wind up working for a *gaijin* company. Moreover, given that the Japanese rarely put subsidiaries or divisions up for sale, we'd have to do some intensive salesmanship to convince Nagase to relinquish what was undeniably a cash cow.

"WE'LL DISCUSS THIS AND GET BACK TO YOU SOON"

103

During our Hawaiian talks at a Sheraton resort located fifty miles northeast of Honolulu, we wanted to convey three important messages to our Japanese distributors. First, that we weren't seeking to disengage with them because they were doing a poor job. If anything, they'd done an excellent job and worked hard for us. We simply needed to integrate marketing and distribution into our overall operation as part of our forward-thinking strategy. As I relayed this idea, Kay Whitmore stood up and reaffirmed how pleased we were with their performance and that we felt the fairest thing to do was to negotiate an equitable price for the distribution networks.

This didn't make Nagase-*san* or Kusuda-*san* feel any better; after several moments of silence, both tried to assure us that we were being premature and could surely work out a new arrangement. Some months later, when it was clear that we did not agree, Nagase-*san's* brother-in-law, Hideo, who sat in on the meeting, told me that if he'd been in charge at the time he would have found our intent so repugnant that he would have angrily stormed out of the room (he did turn beet red when I announced our intentions). Nagase-*san* himself was a very mild-mannered man who had dealt extensively with Westerners, since his customers included GE, DuPont, and others, so although he was upset by the prospect of the deal, he was less likely to find our suggestion "repugnant." Kusuda-*san* later said that he felt as if he had been kicked in the stomach by my announcement, although since then we became good friends and remain so today.

The morning after the infamous dinner, we tried to lighten the mood, but it was clear that our guests were still devastated by our proposal. Our agenda had called for a round of golf and a round of meetings to discuss how we'd proceed with the acquisition plans. The

golf went over all right, but none of our Japanese guests wanted to discuss the acquisition issue. So after the game we sent them back to the airport, leaving us to ponder our next move.

In point of fact, as a Japanese law firm made perfectly clear to us, we had no written contract with either company, so both could claim that they could expect to distribute Kodak's products in the future as well. Disengaging could, in fact, be considerably more difficult than we'd anticipated.

It appeared that we would have an easier time with Kusuda, since only fifty people were involved, and we'd heard through the grapevine that the employees were nervous about the company's future in the highly competitive distribution market.

Fortunately, our hunch was on target, and the Kusuda people were all too glad to come on board a foreign company with deep pockets. The Kusuda acquisition encouraged us and provided valuable leverage that we could use in bringing Nagase to the bargaining table. Prior to the Kusuda acquisition, we had no way of building a distribution network. With Kusuda on board, we'd have a springboard, albeit small, to begin building our channels.

Once Kusuda was a done deal, we began meeting weekly with a Nagase negotiating team. The course that followed illustrates what I later came to recognize as three phases of a typical acquisition (during my stay in Japan, Kodak made numerous other acquisitions that followed a similar pattern):

Phase 1: You can't be serious. Often, the first mention of an acquisition will evoke feelings of incredulity, accompanied by implied or outright feelings of umbrage. The Nagase officials exhibited Phase 1 at the

Sheraton meeting and continued their affront for several meetings, until it was clear that we weren't going to cave in.

Phase 1 feelings are in part caused by the need to save face, which is a sensitive cultural issue throughout Asia. This became clear when we tried to schedule meetings at Kodak. It was no problem calling meetings across town at Nagase's headquarters. But every time we tried to plan for a meeting at Kodak, the Nagase team would become visibly uncomfortable: they simply didn't want others to see them walking into our offices to negotiate the sale of one of their companies. Once we realized what was going on, we simply scheduled all of the meetings to take place on Nagase's home turf. The productivity of the meetings took a remarkable upswing when we did so.

Phase 2: We don't agree to the deal, but if we were to, what would the deal be? The second phase moves the parties from disbelief to a preliminary acceptance of the inevitability of the situation. This involves talking about what the deal *might* amount to *if* it were to happen. We were mired in this stage with Nagase for nearly five months.

During the talks we often found ourselves befuddled by three major cultural differences in negotiating protocol and style. First, while the Nagase people had appointed the head of their negotiating team, one Fujimore-*san*, it was never clear who was actually in charge. This made it difficult to assign weight to each person's contributions to the discussion and relative clout in the decision-making process.

Second, the meetings were often punctuated by long periods of silence (many minutes) and stone faces. For the Japanese, who tend to be very thoughtful people and not prone to thinking out loud, such lulls are perfectly normal. Americans, on the other hand, typically

want to fill in the blanks or sweeten the deal rather than face "down time." So we had to work hard at disciplining ourselves to be able to sit in silence for what seemed like an eternity and wait for a response. (The ability to endure the silence later proved invaluable in negotiating other Japanese deals.)

Finally, when faced with questions that hadn't been discussed among the group, the Nagase team would typically answer, "We'll discuss this and get back to you later." Most new proposals were put off in this way, and we had to accept the fact that if we wanted to make the acquisition, we would have to accept a very long game consisting of slow-motion volleys.

Phase 3: *OK, we'll sign—on the bottom of a one- or two-page agreement.* The final phase moves from abstractions about the potential landscape of the deal to very real and specific proposals. When we got to the point where they'd agreed on the fact that they'd do the deal, they continually cautioned us that they really didn't have the right to transfer employees from one company to another. So we spent another nine months talking about human relations and agreed that to encourage Division for Kodak Products employees to transfer on their own, we would initially establish a joint enterprise, the Kodak/Nagase venture. In three or four years, the entire operation could be turned over to Kodak.

With this final bit of the deal in place—twenty-two months after the Hawaii meeting—Eastman Kodak's Kay Whitmore and an executive VP flew to Tokyo to shake hands with a Nagase president and consummate the deal. The only problem was that the Nagase people wanted to pretty much leave things with a handshake. Oh, they were willing to sign a one- or two-page letter of agreement that ended with the ubiquitous contract closer: "If anything needs to be discussed as circumstances change, both parties will do their best to do so." Once again, the old concept of *gambatte* (trying your best) cropped up, in this case reducing the agreement to good faith.

Of course, Eastman Kodak was not about to agree to a deal of this magnitude by signing a one- or two-page agreement. (We were also especially sensitive to the riskiness of operating without adequate legal protection, given the fact that both distributors could have dug in their heels and insisted on the right to continue to distribute our products. So we retained a corporate Japanese law firm that worked with our U.S.-based lawyers for nine months to draft a document that, when bound into individual notebooks and placed side by side measured five feet in length!

The deal took nearly two-and-a-half years start to finish—not bad, I'm told, for a major transaction. Ironically, while the massive contract met our needs and served as a great showpiece for my office (many people came to ogle the credenza that housed the multi-volume tome), I'm convinced that from Nagase's standpoint, it didn't carry an ounce more authority than the spoken word did!

A simple verbal contract is worth more than reams of paper to your Japanese partners; be prepared for a handshake instead of a tome.

FIGHTING FIRE
WITH FIRE
Playing and Winning at the Keiretsu Game

Irma and I had just stepped out our front door to shop at the local grocery store when we heard, "Albert. Oh, Allllbert!"

I looked around and couldn't believe my eyes. There was my wispy 85-year-old aunt Alice waving from a taxicab window. The driver was two blocks down the street, wildly knocking on doors to find where Sieg-san lived. Auntie had been traveling in China and, since she had my address with her, "swung by" Tokyo on her way home. The hotel clerk translated my address into directions for the cab driver, and with that, Auntie dauntlessly ventured into the suburbs of Tokyo.

My aunt had no idea of the enormous challenge ahead of the cab driver, for the Japanese have very few street names or signs, let alone a logical house numbering system. The first parts of our address were no problem:

Tokyo (city), *Minato-ku* (ward), *Moto Azabu* (town), *2-chome* (section).

The second part,

13-1 (13th ban, first property),

was a lot trickier. The *ban* can be as large as an acre, and the property numbers reflect when the dwelling *site* was first occupied. Ours was the first property to be occupied, so our house number was 1. Our next-door neighbor was number 66, and the house across the street bore the number 132.

This system is extremely disconcerting to non-Japanese, and it's not surprising that one of the first things that the U.S. occupation forces did after World War II was to assign street names and street numbers. The occupation forces also weren't happy about a few other things, not the least of which was the presence of the old family business cartels or *zaibatsu*, which they promptly banned because of their support during the war of the militaristic and imperialistic Japanese government. When the U.S. forces left, the Japanese immediately took down the street signs: they never had any use for them. And they soon formed a new type of business alliances, the *keiretsu*, which more than anything else set Japanese companies apart from those in the West.

The *keiretsu* are interlocking groups of Japanese companies that dominate an area of business. Once a month, the presidents of the companies involved in the *keiretsu* meet to discuss issues affecting the group. Far more than a business association or rotary club, the *keiretsu* are tightly bonded together in spirit and by mutual shareholding. For this reason, some academics define the *keiretsu* as the essence of "relationship capitalism" rather than "independent capitalism."

Each company holds a small quantity of shares of the other members (typically 1 to 2 percent). The shares are bought for the purpose of building relationship capital rather than a capital return on an investment. Although the number of shares involved is far too small to affect the marketplace, the relationship capital they generate serves as a kind of glue that binds the *keiretsu* members together. Even though a company might be able to get a better price on items from a non-*keiretsu* member, it will always buy from its *keiretsu* brother first.

If a *keiretsu* company finds itself in trouble, other members will come to the rescue, often by engineering a bank loan in which an officer of the bank joins the failing company's board. In this way, the *keiretsu* serves as a kind of safety net for member companies.

Finally, the strong relationship capital virtually eliminates the possibility for hostile takeovers, shareholder revolts, leveraged buyouts, and other shareholder actions. When you have 100 to 200 companies in the *keiretsu* holding small vault shares, that doesn't leave a lot of room for a raider or anyone else who wants to gain control through the open market. (T. Boone Pickens was once able to purchase 20 percent of one of Toyota's *keiretsu* member companies through a disgruntled stockholder. But the rest of the shareholders stiff-armed

the Texas raider, refusing him a position on the board, and he eventually abandoned the pursuit.)

Since the rise of the *keiretsu* concept after the war, three types of *keiretsu* associations have evolved: horizontal, vertical, and distribution. The horizontal *keiretsu* is often centered around a major bank and a trading house (marketing and distribution firms). For example, the Mitsubishi *keiretsu* has more than 200 companies associated with it, including the Mitsubishi Bank, the Mitsubishi Trading House, and Mitsubishi Heavy Industries (steel, shipmaking, chemicals, and so on). The vertical *keiretsu* revolves around a major manufacturing company and hundreds of smaller vendors of components and service. The Toyota *keiretsu* is a classic example and includes all of the companies that supply the automaker on a just-in-time basis. Finally, the distribution *keiretsu* consists of a group of factories and distributors.

Now, if all this sounds like major trouble for foreign competition, be assured that it is; officials from the United States, Europe, and other non-Japanese countries have bitterly complained that the cliquish *keiretsu* lock out much of the foreign competition and close off distribution channels to nonmembers. While the Japanese government and major *keiretsu* deny any biases, the debate rages on. Congressman Richard Gephardt summed up the *keiretsu* as the heart of the incompatibility between the U.S. and Japanese economies. Trade representatives find it anti-antitrust and 180 degrees apart from the American way of capitalism. But on the other side, asking the Japanese to open up or do away with their *keiretsu* would be asking them to toss out the system that has served them so well since World War II.

Arguments of antitrust aside, the fact remains that Kodak was shut out of a major portion of the distribution pipeline after World War II

and the rise of the *keiretsu*. We just didn't realize how bad the situation was until we began looking at it firsthand. Fuji—and later members of its vertical *keiretsu*, which owned manufacturing, photofinishing, and other processes—controlled approximately 50 percent of the film distribution channel. Everywhere we turned we'd bump into what appeared to be an attempt to keep our products off the market. And there was no way that we were going to be accepted into Fuji's (or any other *keiretsu*) in the foreseeable future.

Gradually it dawned on us that if we couldn't beat the *keiretsu* or join them, we could fight fire with fire by creating our own mini-*keiretsu* that would include our major photographic customers, especially those being wooed by Fuji. One large business customer, a professional laboratory and film distributor, was on the brink of being won over to Fugi, so we needed to take decisive action. After a number of discussions and drinking sessions with the customer, we all agreed to a cross-shareholding relationship in which Kodak Japan would purchase 3 to 5 percent of the customer's stock. It, in turn, would purchase a token amount of Kodak shares.

The cross-shareholding meant to the Japanese world that we'd formed an alliance in which we would work together as customer and supplier. To Fuji, it was a strong signal to forget about pursuing this particular customer. Fuji understood and respected the game rules of business alliances, and even though our *keiretsu* was an American knock-off, it gave up pursuing our member partner as a prospect.

The "shark repellent" was so effective that we wanted to form cross-shareholding arrangements with other companies and fully protect our turf. Unfortunately, while the ideas of a mini-*keiretsu* made

perfect sense from our vantage point, the corporate office back in Rochester was not thrilled with the idea of tying up more cash in other people's companies for cross-shareholding. Also, our lawyers back in the States were having panic attacks about whether such arrangements were violations of U.S. antitrust laws.

After much negotiating with Rochester, I finally convinced headquarters that even if the company could do better in the short term by investing the money elsewhere, the long-term payoff would be far greater. Then there was always the flip side of the equation: if we didn't do something along the lines that we were proposing to secure our best customers, our entire operation base in Japan could erode permanently. Rochester finally agreed, and after the lawyers convinced themselves that there were no antitrust problems, we were able to bring more customers into our mini-*keiretsu* fold, as well as a large manufacturer of photofinishing equipment.

When I was preparing to leave Japan in the early 1990s, quasi-*keiretsu* and business alliances were popping up all over the place, as large companies that were successful globally, such as DuPont, realized that Japan is a special place and no company can survive by itself regardless of how large and powerful it may be.

About the same time, the real *keiretsu* were beginning to weaken because of Japan's recession and "asset deflation." Many of the banks in the most powerful *keiretsu* had tied up their assets in the stock market and land holdings, both of which took a tumble as the bubble economy of the 1970s and 1980s finally burst. So the banks lost some of their flexibility to fund the *keiretsu* activities and bail out sinking members.

Even so, the *keiretsu* are here to stay and will likely always pose a formidable hurdle for Western and other foreign companies. But I

suspect that the mini-*keiretsu* concept that we started at Kodak will survive too.

Hey, if my Auntie Alice could take a whirlwind tour at age eighty-five and find her way to a city with no street names, anything is possible!

When it comes to keiretsu, if you can't beat 'em, join 'em. If you can't join 'em, copy 'em!

AKIHABARA
How the Japanese Conduct Real-Time Market Research

I looked longingly at the Matsushita electric bread maker in the vendor's stall, but I knew Irma was right: if we added one more countertop appliance to our Lilliputian kitchen, we wouldn't have enough space left to cook a single ramen noodle. Oh, but the smell of fresh bread—there's nothing on earth sweeter to me. I glanced back at the rectangular device as we made our way to the next vendor stall, imagining how nicely it would fit on our aircraft-carrier-sized kitchen counter back in Rochester. . . .

If it runs on batteries or can be plugged into an electric socket, you'll find it on display at Akihabara. What started in the late 1940s as a collection of open-air peddlers who sold surplus World War II radio parts is now the world's largest display of consumer electronic goods, sprawling over a square mile of bustling downtown Tokyo. Today, vendors at Akihabara's nearly 500 stalls and stores sell everything from components and camcorders to rice cookers and washing machines. Computer gear has been the hot ticket at Akihabara since the early 1990s and will probably continue to be a major item for many years to come.

On the small-scale side of the bazaar, some vendors operate out of six- by ten-foot stalls crammed solid with goods. Many of these peddlers specialize in a particular type of component or electronic esoterica, such as memory modules, transformers, or switches. Visit a computer hard-disk stall and you can choose from hundreds of sizes and models. The same holds for other components, making Akihabara a paradise for hobbyists and small manufacturing companies with, say, one to five people, as well as those who enjoy poking around well-stocked, old-fashioned hardware stores: Akihabara is the hardware store of the electronic age.

Other small vendors at Akihabara specialize in finished products, such as portable tape or CD players and other personal electronic items. It's a window shopper's dream come true, if you can stand the shock of wading through so many choices.

At the large-scale extreme of Akihabara, you'll find six- to eight-story buildings stocked with a dizzying array of electronic gear, all organized by floors. The first floor of a typical megastore might feature 500 television sets ranging in size from three-inch personal

models to "monster screens" probably bigger than the walls of typical Japanese dwellings. The store might devote the next floor to stereo equipment and offer people the opportunity to compare hundreds of different speakers in acoustically-engineered listening rooms. Other floors might feature boom boxes and radios or miniature refrigerators, stoves, and other appliances geared for single use in typical Japanese apartments. (It's amazing to see customers struggling to get on board public transportation from Akihabara with a large television set or small refrigerator—somehow they manage!)

Whether you visit a few stalls or tour the megastores, you'll find a carnival-like atmosphere at Akihabara, with hawkers trying to yell above blaring background music and thousands of pieces of booming audio gear. Neon signs atop the taller buildings add to the playful ambiance by bathing the ground below in garish colored light. But the business that gets transacted at Akihabara is serious stuff: according to the *Wall Street Journal* as much as 10 percent of all of Japan's sales of electrical appliances and consumer electronic equipment take place within Akihabara's stores and stalls.

The high level of business activity isn't surprising considering that tens of millions of people visit the shops at Akihabara every year. Even during a "slow" period, shoppers have to pick their way through massive crowds. But no one seems to mind; whereas crowds in the United States get testy, even downright dangerous, if contained for too long, the Japanese have come to accept crowds as a simple fact of living in one of the most densely populated countries on the planet. To really appreciate this adaptation, just visit Akihabara on a rainy day and observe how thousands of people maneuver around each other with umbrellas; some hold their umbrellas at four feet, some at five

feet, and others at six feet. They instinctively pick the right height for ensuring the free-flow of traffic, just as airline controllers designate the right altitude for planes going to and fro in various air corridors throughout the country.

In addition to being a shopper's paradise, Akihabara serves as the Japanese electronic industry's "real-time market-research site." Not that many Japanese businesspeople would explain it quite in those terms; market research has never been big in Japan. The Japanese have only about 20 percent the number of market research firms that you'll find in the United States, and most are actually subsidiaries of advertising agencies that exist for the purpose of supporting ad campaigns. Akio Morita, Sony Corporation's leader, even goes on to say in his book, *Made in Japan,* that he didn't believe any amount of market research could have told his company that the Walkman could be so successful.

While I believe in the power of good market research for products already on the shelf, I'm not entirely confident about research for goods still under development. People really can't give you useful information about a product until they can see it, touch it, and play with it. And that's where Akihabara comes in. Consumers can see and hold cutting-edge electronic goods and provide instant feedback to the sales reps. Frequently, the sales reps aren't from the sales department at all: they're engineers who are capable of asking important questions and then going back to the drawing board to transform customer reactions into critical fixes and modifications. In other words, Akihabara allows the Japanese to gather instant feedback and fold it into their product development efforts. Here's my take on how it all works:

1. Design a product.

2. Make a few prototypes, then have your engineers demo them at Akihabara and ask customers for their opinion (it's not all market research; the idea is to clinch as many sales as you can, too).

3. Take note of requested features and problem fixes.

4. Bring back next-generation or enhanced models and see how customers like them.

5. Repeat this process until the product is perfected.

6. Have the factory flip into warp drive and flood the global marketplace.

This represents the "fuzzy logic" or "continuous-feedback loop" approach so characteristic of Japanese research and development. While the Western straight-line approach rushes a project from idea to production (often leading to products that consumers don't want or products that are too flawed for "prime time"), the Japanese are willing to endure many iterations before committing to a full-scale roll-out.

In addition to evolving products through outlets such as Akihabara, some companies use a subsidiary as a guinea pig to gain the rapid feedback that will afford them a competitive edge. Matsushita, for example, often uses its cutting-edge JVC subsidiary for this purpose; when the technology is ironed out, the electronics giant gears up for production and storms the marketplace. (It also helps to have your

own major chain of retail stores, as Matsushita does. Initially, the company places a few cutting-edge products in each store and sees how actual buyers—not just window shoppers—respond. They know that if Japanese customers are unhappy, they aren't reluctant to come back to the point of sale and express their feelings.)

While we never had occasion to take anything back to Akihabara, we did enjoy the experience of window shopping there, despite the wall-to-wall crowds and the difficulty in finding food (which is uncharacteristic for most urban areas in Japan; as an old saying goes, Japan is a land of restaurants every fifty feet and a sake bar in between). Sometimes it was fun to go for the sneak preview of a new technology or to purchase goods (other than bread makers) that we planned to ship home.

Regardless of the motivation for the excursion, we'd always take the *Yamanote* line, an elevated train that completely encircles Tokyo, to the Akihabara stop and experiment with a different way of entering the bazaar. One time we made our way in through a nondescript back door on a side street and found ourselves in a small room in one of the big electronics stores, Musen Radio Co. (a name that reflects Akihabara's celebrated past). About ten people were getting a demo of digital audio tape, or DAT, a full two years before American audiophiles would have their first glimpse of the newest recording technology. The demonstration was a combination of customer education and real-time market research, with the sales engineer asking questions of the audience such as, "How do you feel the DAT tape sound compares to CD? Do you think it's as convenient to operate? Would you like to be able to record at CD-level quality? And would you pay X yen for a DAT player?"

Purists might say all this is a matter of semantics—that the Japanese are simply running focus groups in disguise. I disagree and believe that there's a fundamental difference between the market-research mentality of American companies and the Japanese approach to using customer feedback on a real-time basis. Focus groups are by definition artificial; real-time feedback is garnered through one-on-one interactions. Moreover, the goal of a focus group is simply to walk away with information. While real-time feedback does generate information, it will also hopefully lead to a sale, which is the ultimate litmus test of whether a product has potential in the marketplace.

Since the Japanese are always interested in feedback from *gaijin*, it usually didn't take long before a salesperson would approach me to demo a new product or technology during one of my Akihabara forays. (I quickly learned that salespeople who didn't speak English would do anything to avoid eye contact with me so they wouldn't waste time trying to communicate through ad hoc sign language.) I would always try to provide useful feedback, and at the end of the demo the salesperson would always try to sell me a unit—but never in a high-pressure way. Pushing product is simply not what Akihabara (or any other selling outlet in Japan) is all about.

Throughout my stay in Japan I visited Akihabara at least a dozen times, and my only regret was that Irma held fast on her bread maker veto (we did subsequently purchase a countertop unit when we returned home). But then I accidentally discovered something almost as good: a subway stop located right next to a bakery. As I walked the 100 or more stairs to street level, the aroma of fresh bread grew

stronger with each step. This, I said to myself, must truly be the stairway to heaven.

You don't need abstractions like QFD or "Voice of the Customer" to understand what consumers want; just follow the Japanese lead of on-the-spot, real-time feedback.

INCREMENTAL
IMPROVEMENT
Pursuing the Right Thing to Do

When Inai-san granted our request for a visit to his factories on Shikoku Island, my colleagues and I had no idea that he intended for us to tour all the plants on the island. We only discovered his ambitious tour plans while en route by minibus from the second to the third plant, which was located twenty miles out in the country. "We have to be back tomorrow afternoon," I said to the driver. "It doesn't seem possible for us to visit eleven more factories between now and tomorrow morning."

"Not to worry, Sieg-san," the driver assured me. As we pulled into the parking lot of plant number three, he grinned and pointed to the rooftop where Inai-san's personal helicopter sat perched like a praying mantis. "This really is going to be a

whirlwind island tour!" I said to my colleagues who joined me
for the trip. The pun didn't translate well, but at least I could
stop fretting about the schedule and enjoy the rest of the visit.

Japanese companies constantly visit each other to learn about ways of
boosting productivity and efficiency. And while no company gives
away trade secrets when hosting a tour, most are remarkably open
about showing visitors how they excel in their various niches. While
I had participated in several factory tours and enjoyed a great
deal of respect, I was not prepared for Inai-*san*'s all-out red-carpet
treatment.

Known locally as the "Emperor of Shikoku," Inai-*san* reigned over
Matsushita Kotobuki, a subsidiary of the giant Matsushita Industrial
Electric. His division, which sprawled over thirteen facilities on Japan's fifth island, manufactured VCRs, camcorders, and a variety of
consumer electronic products sold under Matsushita's and several
other subsidiary labels. A close associate and friend of Matsushita
Konosuke, the legendary guru of Japanese manufacturing philosophy
and technique, Inai-*san* himself was greatly respected in the world of
Japanese manufacturing. He was also known for his hospitality—
reflected in the lavish hotel accommodations he provided and the
banquet he threw in our honor, which included more courses of
Japanese food than I'd ever seen placed on a table at one time.

During the two-day tour of Matsushita Kotobuki, we spent an hour
at each factory, beginning with the facility that makes components
and ending with the final assembly plants where chassis and parts

magically come together as finished products. The final assembly plant was a brilliant example of Japanese know-how and a testimony to the power of *kaizen* or incremental change. The last plant we visited had four assembly lines that were used to manufacture VCRs. The lines started at the east end of the building and then ran for several hundred feet to the west end (because of limited development and a sparse population, space was not a big problem on the island of Shikoku as it was elsewhere in Japan, so the plants tended to be more on the scale of those found in the West). As each VCR-in-process made its way down the line, it would "grow" from individual subassemblies until it was a completed unit. At that point, the line would double back on an elevated track and return to the east end, where a label would be affixed to the front and the units would be wrapped, placed in a box, then packaged for shipping.

As the VCRs passed through various stations, they were subject to a battery of rigorous quality tests, as well as environmental tests, to ensure that they operated properly within their specified temperature ranges. Although the line ran smoothly during the tour, Inai-*san* proudly explained that if any problems are encountered, they're solved on the spot. Unlike the traditional American line, in which problems are solved after the fact, resulting in piles of defective goods and scrap, Inai-*san*'s factories showed almost no signs of waste.

Perhaps the most amazing thing about the odyssey from loose parts to finished product was the fact that each line was operated by just *two* people! While a highly skilled engineering staff was constantly tweaking the automated stations and robotic arms, the two line workers really ran the whole show. When Inai-*san* saw the look of astonishment on my face, he laughed and, through his interpreter, told me that if I'd visited the plant five years ago, I would have seen hundreds of people assembling the VCRs together by hand. "That was during the innovation stage," he explained, "when engineers studied how the VCRs came together and then automated each stage of the process, using the concept of *kaizen* to move the production line from manual assembly to full automation, stage-by-stage." Once the first line was automated, he said, the company moved the people on to a new start-up line for another product so that the engineers could study the procedures and begin automating them as well.

As we boarded the minivan for the return trip to the airport, Inai said, "As proud as I am of this process, if you come back in another year, you'll be amazed at the improvements. We never let a day go by without making incremental improvement in the process. We have an unrelenting, inexhaustible quest for making incremental improvements in our processes."

Those words stuck with me throughout my entire stay in Japan and essentially turned my understanding of manufacturing on its head. Whenever I visited a company, I looked for other examples where the use of incremental improvement had led to significant gains in productivity and reductions in cost. Both were evident at the Chinon plant that was manufacturing what at the time was the world's smallest computer printer. Eastman Kodak had purchased Mead Paper's ink-jet division (which Kodak renamed "Diconex") and also bought a substantial interest in Chinon, Inc. Kodak believed that Chinon would be able to take Mead's ink-jet design and render it into a miniature printer that was not only manufacturable but could be produced at a cost-per-value ratio that would greatly appeal to customers.

Like Matsushita, Chinon began with manual assembly lines that engineers observed and then later automated. I was able to see the evolution from fully manual lines to fully automated production lines over the course of the year as I made routine site visits of the Chinon plant (my presidential duties included routine inspections of various Kodak production facilities).

Step by step, the manual process of assembling a Diconex printer became automated—except one operation, which involved placing a belt on a gear. This was done by a solitary worker assigned to the belt station. On the fourth visit, however, I noticed that the application of the belt was being done by a robot hand—a very deft robot hand, at that. The hand would first insert its fingers inside a belt, slightly stretch the elastic material, then place the belt over a set of spindles on the printer gear. The entire process was truly elegant.

During my visit, I had the good fortune of watching Chinon's engineering team work on the robot hand. After observing the engineers, I asked why Chinon had decided to take the final incremental step in converting from a manual system to an automated production line. "Did you make the decision after calculating the labor you'd save and running a return-on-investment analysis?" I inquired as I looked over their shoulders. The engineers were confused by my question, perhaps even a bit insulted. "No, Sieg-*sacho*," they replied. "It has been our team's experience that when tasks and processes get automated, tasks and processes get better. So it was simply the right thing to do."

I understood. And I was eager to apply *kaizen* at Kodak. The timing was certainly ripe; in 1987, Kodak decided to build its first manufacturing operation in Japan. We had previously entered the Japanese market by selling product made abroad through third-party distributors,

but by the mid-1980s it became clear that additional profits were to be made by manufacturing product right on the island.

We focused our planning on the graphic arts side of the business, which sold numerous products to the printing industry, such as negatives for making printing plates and film for converting color pictures into color lithographs used in books and magazines. Since Japanese graphic arts customers used different-sized films than those made for U.S. companies, we couldn't just import stock products. Rather, we brought in U.S.-sized product produced at Kodak's plants outside Japan, then hired a third party to recut the product into the correct Japanese sizes. This subcontracting took a substantial bite out of Kodak's profits, since "finishing" (cutting and packaging) could amount to 40 percent of the overall cost of a particular film product.

We were easily able to justify the construction of a small finishing plant, to which we could later add more manufacturing capabilities. Corporate sanctioned the plan and supplied industrial engineering help from Kodak Park in Rochester, New York to help us design the factory and choose the equipment we'd need. We also worked out an arrangement with the Park whereby we'd send six outstanding people from one of our photo processing facilities to Rochester for eight to ten weeks of intensive hands-on training in film finishing.

At first blush, it might seem that cutting and packing film into specified sizes doesn't require a Ph.D. in materials science. In fact, there's a real art to the job. First, there's the issue of making the most efficient use of the master roll, which measures five feet wide and several thousand feet long. With the aid of a computer, you have to figure out how to cut the film into all the required odd sizes with a minimum of waste. The cuts, which are done with a sophisticated

piece of machinery, must be incredibly precise, the tolerances being plus zero and minus one-ten-thousandth of an inch. To add to the challenge, all the cutting and packing must be done in total darkness, or the film will be ruined!

Despite the intricacies of finishing film, four weeks after our Japanese team had left for the States, I received a phone call from their manager, who said, "These guys have everything they need to know about finishing. There's no need to keep them in the Park any longer—unless they'd like to stay here permanently and work for us." This was not surprising to me. The Japanese are "superlearners" who have an incredible ability to soak up information: their whole school system is based on the acquisition of vast amounts of facts. I don't think any other culture has refined memorization to such a high degree.

When my trainees returned to Tokyo (I breathed a sigh of relief that they weren't enticed into staying on in Rochester), we ordered the finishing equipment for our plant. Much of the gear was nonstandard, so we had to place special orders that would take up to several months to fill. Meanwhile our finishing team began looking at the proposed layout and evaluated it against their experiences at Kodak Park. They humbly offered numerous suggestions for improving the flow of work and overall efficiency, all of which we took very seriously. For example, they recommended removing many of the "buffers" between work stations. As planned, product would be temporarily inventoried or stored "off-line" as it moved from machine to machine. Their ideas for rearranging the flow of material made a great deal of sense and would lead to a considerably more efficient operation, not to mention the elimination of space for storing unnecessary work-in-process.

Once the plant was on line, the original trainee group passed its knowledge onto new hires who would operate the equipment and continued to make suggestions for incrementally improving the finishing processes. Without our directing them to do so, the group met regularly for morning meetings during which they discussed problems and improvement opportunities. They were truly driven by that "unrelenting, inexhaustible quest for making incremental improvements" that Inai-*san* attributed to his companies' success.

We could point to *kaizen* for our success, too. Not only did the finishing plant begin operation right on schedule and underbudget, but through steady, small changes it had achieved a level of productivity that we hadn't expected to see for at least eighteen months. And quality was as good or better than that found at any other Kodak finishing site in the entire world.

Always look for opportunities for "the right thing to do." You never know when they'll lead to major process breakthroughs.

INNOVATORS IN THE MIDST

Dispelling the No-Creativity-Here Myth

Hayakawa-san could hardly contain himself when he heard the news: the next molecular beam epitaxy unit to roll off the assembly line would be ours! I, too, was surprised, as we had been emphatically told that we'd have to wait at least two years to receive our order. What bumped us up to position number one? Without realizing it, we'd hired one of the world's leading experts on molecular beam epitaxy, and the company that made the epitaxy processing machine certainly didn't want to keep this eminent scientist waiting!

Soon after completing our research lab in Yokohama, we decided to begin doing the kind of long-term theoretical work that could eventually have big payoffs, particularly in the semiconductors used to convert light into electronic imagery. One technique for creating such semiconductors, molecular beam epitaxy, looked particularly promising. The process involved the precise placement of an atom or a molecule of semiconductor material on a slice of silicon. This represented a major improvement over standard "evaporative" techniques for creating layered semiconductors; with the evaporative techniques, it was much more difficult to control the thickness of the component or where the semiconductor atoms or molecules would land. Molecular beam epitaxy is incredibly precise and allows for the creation of all kinds of new semiconductors based on a variety of materials.

The only problem with molecular beam epitaxy was that it was still just a theoretical process, and we didn't have the expertise within Kodak to bring it from the lab bench to the production line. So we turned to a headhunting firm to help us find a scientist who had the right background for helping us to commercialize the technique. The firm had just the man we'd been looking for—one Hayakawa-*san*, who had been working on molecular beam epitaxy for some years in a Japanese competitor's lab. (I considered it a high-level compliment that Japanese headhunters would even consider placing their top prospects with a foreign capital firm.) Hayakawa-*san* had already read about our new laboratory facility in Yokohama and was very attracted to the freewheeling research culture characteristic of Western-style companies.

After two interviews, Hayakawa-*san* was ready to sign with Kodak, and a month later, he reported for duty. About that time, we placed an

order with the VG Corporation, the world's leading maker of molecu-lar beam epitaxy processing equipment. We built into our schedule the fact that we'd probably have to wait a good two years before the extremely expensive unit would be shipped and installed, so it was with great delight that we were informed about receiving the next unit off the assembly line—because of Hayakawa-*san*'s reputation.

While we knew that Hayakawa-*san* had done extensive research in the area and was well regarded in the field, his worldwide preeminence and influence in academic and commercial circles was nevertheless surprising to us. First, it would have been hard to guess the man's status in the scientific community from his humble demeanor. A fence rail of a fellow whose eyes always seemed abnormally large through the thick lenses of his wire-rim glasses, he never thought of himself as above his fellow researchers. He was also a natural teacher, always eager to explain molecular beam epitaxy to anyone who would listen.

Second, as a Westerner, I'd simply assumed that the Japanese tend to be great at copying and refining technology, rather than making breakthrough discoveries. Many Westerners assume that the Japanese approach to research, based on *kaizen* or incremental improvement, runs counter to the innovation process because it doesn't encourage people to think in terms of "sea changes" or major breakthroughs. They also point to the traditional Japanese style of managing research as being "anti-innovative." Unlike Western-style labs, which promote individual creativity, Japanese labs expect that the individual will subordinate himself (virtually all technical people in Japan are men) to the group, that the group will solve problems, and that the group will be responsible for technical advancements.

Now, it's true that during its post–World War II recovery period,

Japan explicitly avoided reinventing the wheel, instead borrowing technologies that others had invented. And in some cases, Western companies were all too glad to license technologies to Japanese firms, figuring that they'd never be a competitive threat. But the record shows that the Japanese have been on the cutting edge in many technology areas, such as ceramics and semiconductors. In fact, during the past ten years, Japanese companies have been among the top ten patent recipients. Not every patent is of the importance of, say, the transistor, but creative gears in Japan are turning very rapidly and producing exciting new materials and products. (Ironically, just as the United States is cutting back its R&D investment, Japan is revving up its R&D budget and investing heavily in Western-style facilities in America and other countries.)

Given the Japanese ability to do cutting-edge research, it's no wonder that companies such as DuPont, IBM, Xerox, and Hewlett-Packard have built substantial R&D facilities in Japan to take advantage of the country's brainpower and creativity. And it's also no wonder that the VG Corporation didn't want our man, Hayakawa-*san*, an innovator of molecular beam epitaxy technology, to wait two years for the latest processing unit, since it was based on his theoretical insights.

When the epitaxy device did arrive, it caused quite a commotion in the research lab, if for no other reason than its unusual appearance. A bright metallic chamber measuring about eight feet by six feet and sporting numerous tubes, valves, and protuberances, the processing unit looked more like a contraption designed for exploring the bottom of the sea or the Martian polar caps than a piece of semiconductor research apparatus. During the month of installation, under Hayakawa-*san's* supervision, people from all corners of the

facility came to examine the exotic-looking piece of gear and learn about its use.

Once the epitaxy unit was operational, we gave Hayakawa-*san* a great deal of latitude in terms of what he could do with it. And while he still had much theoretical work ahead of him in terms of understanding the epitaxy process, Hayakawa-*san* felt driven to find practical applications as quickly as possible. Like many Japanese researchers, he had an innate compunction to do something useful and spent a fair amount of work time trying to actually produce semiconductors that would end up in commercial products. One of the many components he created was a blue-light-emitting semiconductor that could be extremely useful in developing color laser printers and other important products. The list could go on and on, but the fact remains the same: Hayakawa-*san* didn't fit the stereotype and serves as a living lesson to anyone who writes off Japan as a land of *takumina mane*—mere imitators.

Creativity can often be found where you least expect it in Japan—keep an open mind and you'll likely stumble upon it.

OF PERFECT WEDDINGS AND PERFECT FISH

Creating Products for Japan

The New Year party was a stunning success, judging from the 600 smiling faces in the room. I positioned myself near one of the doorways while a young woman who worked at the hotel stood behind me holding a tall pole capped with a red crepe ball. The idea was to make me easily discernible to anyone who wanted to exchange a greeting or business card with me. Toward the end of the evening a stocky man in his fifties walked up and placed his card on a nearby tray. I then handed him my card.

"Excuse me," he said politely. "I've been using your films in our studio for twenty-five years, and I want to continue using them for the next twenty-five years. But you're making it difficult for me to do so. My customers are very unhappy and are urging me to start using Fuji's films. What can you do to remedy the situation?"

That was precisely what we wanted to know. We'd heard similar complaints from too many other customers since we began trying to figure out why our ability to sell film in the consumer markets had deteriorated to such an appallingly low level. Because we had sold through third-party distributors for the past forty years, we never got the kind of firsthand feedback that was essential to satisfying our customers—feedback like the kind that Hatano-*san* offered us at the New Year party. So one of our highest priorities after establishing our official operations in Japan was to send a team into the field to talk with customers and find out how we could better serve their needs.

The biggest problem, we learned, was that our film had the wrong color balance for the Japanese marketplace. That was a crucial mistake because people don't really purchase rolls of film; they purchase the color prints that they hope to get back. And the prints that Japanese customers picked up from their local photo finishers were often disappointing: the colors weren't "vivid" (saturated) enough and the images weren't "clear" (sharp) enough, when compared to Fuji's products.

Three months after we began our on-site market research, we presented our findings to the corporate headquarters and R&D labs in Rochester, New York, hoping for a fix to the problem. Instead, we were met with surprise and disbelief that one particular market could be so different from the rest of the world. Fortunately, enough was at stake in Japan that the company made a serious effort to develop a film that would be more suited to the Japanese market, and a year later (a fairly short development cycle for a new film product), we were ready to return with Kodacolor HR, which replaced the Kodacolor II we'd been selling for years. The HR product featured new technology for

sharper images, a better color balance, and improved color saturation.

We then took the improved film to Japan and launched a massive marketing, advertising, and PR campaign to let people know that the contents of the "yellow box" had changed. About the same time, we introduced a new line of professional films for the wedding market, aimed at studios like Hatano-*san's*. The films we'd been exporting were color balanced for Caucasians, the majority of whom have hair on the brown side of the spectrum. Being slightly on the "warmish" side, our films would tend to make the hair of Japanese women turn slightly lighter than the jet-black that it really was. If the photographers tried to compensate with filters, their wedding dresses would come out pinkish, and in Japan, as in America, brides wear *only* white. Trying to compensate for the pinkness of the dress in turn would lead to red hair, and further compensation for that would lead to other unacceptable color problems.

The solution was to create a modified product for the Japanese market so that hair would come out black while dresses remained white. Even though this necessitated the creation of another product in the line, we eagerly went ahead because of the importance of the Japanese marketplace. If we hadn't made the effort, chances are that we'd have lost our market share completely. Also, not catering to the special needs of the wedding market would have undermined our comeback in the consumer market. We had to convince the Japanese that Kodak truly cared about their needs.

Many companies learn the hard way, as we did, that you can't always sell the Japanese on products that work well elsewhere in the world. General Foods discovered this when it attempted to introduce the concept of instant cake mix in Japan. GF figured that everyone has a rice cooker, so why not sell people on the concept of using the rice cooker to make cakes? What the food giant missed was that rice has a very special meaning in Japan and that the idea of making a cake mix in a rice cooker was almost sacrilegious—even for those who didn't have strong feelings about rice. For those who weren't offended, the idea of cleaning the rice cooker after making a cake was rather unpleasant. Not surprisingly, the cake mix was a total dud, and General Foods pulled out of the market.

Unilever had a similar experience when it introduced its All Temperature Cheer in Japan. The product's main selling feature—its adaptability to water of different temperatures—was of no appeal to the Japanese because they wash clothes in only one temperature—cold. So much for Cheer's marketing edge.

Another consumer products maker, Procter & Gamble, was able to create a substantial presence in the Japanese marketplace by reformulating and refining a number of its products that sold well in the West. The company's strategy was facilitated by a strong awareness that Japanese homemakers had different demands for detergents and other products than their American counterparts.

Coca-Cola also understood the importance of *nihonteki*—made *for* Japan—and reaped enormous rewards. In 1988, it made more profit in Japan than it did in the United States! The company did this by creating fifty-seven different brands for the Japanese market, many of them coffees designed to be sold in cans in the ubiquitous vending machines (in every configuration of cream, milk, sugar, hot, cold, and so on). Sold under the "Georgia Coffee" label, the products are second only to the company's soda in terms of generating revenues.

THE TOKYO CHRONICLES

The makers of Coke also tapped into the lucrative health drink market. Virtually every street vendor sells a vitamin-laced health drink designed to give people a boost of energy so they can "do their best," even after a bad night of after-hours drinking.

While some products made for Japan will not be saleable anywhere else in the world, others may have global appeal. In our case, market tests of Kodak HR revealed that the film was extremely popular worldwide—even preferable to Kodacolor II. So as HR evolved, it became Kodak's standard print film offering, and its most recent incarnation, "Gold," is the Kodak product you'll find anywhere in the world where film is sold.

Unfortunately, most companies don't do it right the first time, and before they can leverage their experience in making products for Japan, they have to go through five unpleasant stages:

1. *Denial.* "We haven't had that kind of comment and complaint about our product from anyone else in any part of the world. What's wrong with those people over there?"

2. *The quick fix.* "We'll send out a technical S.W.A.T. team to straighten things out." The tech people spend two or three weeks in Japan and come back saying, "Gee, there is a problem. Let's propose a quick fix until we can convince the powers that be that we need to develop a long-term answer for this market." In our case, that meant trying to persuade people to use various compensating filters, an idea that didn't go over too well with many Japanese photographers.

3. *Top brass buy-in.* Top management sanctions the development of a new or reformulated product, and the folks in R&D and manufacturing gear up for the task ahead.

4. *Relaunch.* When the product is ready, marketing has to reconvince the Japanese public that the reformulated or redesigned product really is made for them.

5. *Pain and suffering.* You take a bath until the buying public is ready to offer you its trust.

It's easy to fall into the trap of assuming that since you have the best products, the best service, and the best price in your own market, the Japanese will beat a path to your door. But it's also easy to avoid the mistake by thoroughly understanding the ways in which the Japanese are similar to us and the ways in which they're different. American car makers, for instance, need to think of the critical service component as well as quality and styling if they're going to make serious inroads into the Japanese market. Ford understood this when it linked up with Mazda to establish the Autorama, a dealer network spanning Japan that enables owners of Ford cars to receive countrywide service. This no doubt made it easier for the 1994 Mustang to become a car of choice.

Finally, whatever the product, it's important to take a long-term view. Including development time, it took more than two years before our first made-for-Japan product caught on and reversed our decline in the marketplace. That's small change compared to how much time Chilean firms spent trying to pry open the door to Japanese kitchens. After nine years of growing salmon on fish farms, they finally per-

fected a fish that was acceptable to the Japanese palate in terms of texture and taste. Today, Chile is the largest producer of fish for Japan, and its long-term view has paid off with a feast of riches.

Whether you're selling film or fish, respect the fact that the Japanese demand unique products geared for their unique culture.

AND NOW A WORD FROM OUR SPONSOR
Creating Ads for Japanese Consumers

Lights, camera, action! A Japanese woman in a one-piece deep-blue swimsuit walks beside a pool filled with equally deep-blue water. The ladders are painted blue, as are the various pieces of poolside furniture. The woman walks up a short series of steps to a low diving board, then with perfect grace plunges into the pool. The equilibrium of the water is hardly disturbed as her lithe body cuts a clean circle in the surface. Meanwhile, an off-camera voice chants the word blue, like a pleasant mantra, to a melodious tune. Suddenly the woman resurfaces and the camera zooms in on her face, her jet black hair swept back to reveal her blue lipstick, blue eyeliner, and blue eyeshadow. For a brief moment an English voice says, "Kodak is color," and the scene changes to a still picture of a box of Kodak film and Eastman Kodak's corporate logo.

Such was our "blue" spot, one of four ads in our "Kodak is color" campaign. The ads, each devoted to a primary color, were instrumental in helping us to successfully introduce our new "made-for-Japan" color films. Good thing they worked, too, because the new films were a you-bet-the-company kind of gamble to win back Kodak Japan's dwindling marketshare. The ad campaign was an immediate hit and, combined with other marketing programs, showed Kodak in a whole new light. As frosting on the cake, the ads won the top Japanese awards in various categories, an honor not often bestowed on foreign firms. But the road to success on the advertising battlefield was not easily traveled and took no small amount of trial-and-error learning.

Initially, advertising hadn't been part of our Japan strategy. But in 1984, when we actually evaluated our situation in Japan firsthand and began getting direct feedback from customers, we were astounded by the low recognition in what we thought was our major stronghold in the marketplace: the young Japanese consumer. So we undertook a broad series of actions to raise the awareness of the Kodak name among Japanese consumers in general, and consumers in the ten- to twenty-year-old age range, in particular. This included flying the *Kodak Go* blimp around the countryside, building and strategically placing neon signs, listing ourselves on the Tokyo stock exchange, and sponsoring technical and scientific seminars, sumo wrestling matches, judo tournaments, soccer leagues, and the All Japan Junior Tennis Tournament (we were the sole sponsor for the latter event). In addition, we "painted Japan yellow" by putting point-of-purchase and store displays everywhere we could. And we also decided to take to the airwaves and embark on an ambitious advertising campaign.

Like most Western firms, we came to Japan not understanding the

vast differences between ads that would appeal to Americans and Europeans and ads that would "strike a responsive chord" with the Japanese. Western ads invariably focus on the product—its features, its functions, why it's superior, and how it will make you a more efficient, wiser, better-looking, sexier, and all-around happier human being.

In Japan, 80 percent of the ad focuses almost exclusively on the company because Japanese consumers are very conscious about who makes the products they buy. If the company projects a strong, quality image, then by association its products and services must be of high quality as well. So the goal of advertising is to sell people on the company first, the products second. That's why in a typical fifteen-second spot only about three seconds are dedicated to the product—as in our case, where we flashed a picture of the new film box along with the corporate logo.

Not only is the focus of Japanese ads 180 degrees away from Western commercials, but the whole style of communicating is different as well. In the West, advertisers rely heavily on words; in Japan, where language is less expressive, advertisers create moods through ambiance, inference, imagery, music, and so on. Japanese ads focus on the *way* things are said rather than *what* is being said. All this goes toward convincing the consumer that there should be a good feeling between them and the company.

The differences in these two advertising approaches were driven home to me when I attended a cross-cultural session sponsored by the Japanese office of our corporate advertising agency, J. Walter Thompson. The Thompson people held a screening session during which ads made for the United States were shown to Japanese viewers, and vice versa. The Japanese were bemused and befuddled by what they saw; when shown Japanese ads, the Americans snickered.

No wonder that so many Western-style ad campaigns flop when imported to Japan. Likewise, it's not terribly surprising that the reverse is true. For instance, take the ads that accompanied the introduction of the Infiniti automobile in the United States and that were the butt of so many American jokes. The Infiniti executives were baffled by the American response to the beautiful nature scenes that dominated the ads; after all, wouldn't car buyers, sensing the great beauty associated with the company, also ascribe great beauty and other desirable qualities with the car? Not in America!

In order to avoid such mistakes, we knew we'd need the help of a good advertising agency. We probably would have chosen Dentsu, the largest advertising agency in Japan (and by revenues, probably the largest in the world) because they controlled the most air time. Japanese television networks sell time to the ad agencies, which in turn sell it to their clients. Because of its size and clout, Dentsu virtually owned the airwaves. Unfortunately, it was also the agency for our arch rival, Fuji Photo Film. Although Dentsu assured us that its people would build a "Chinese Wall" between the two companies, we simply weren't comfortable with the situation. So we instead turned to J. Walter Thompson's Tokyo office to create a concept that would resonate with a Japanese audience. While Thompson had far less air space to sell us, it was known for its creative work and had served the company well back in the States.

Thompson proved itself to us after developing a series of ads that revolved around a well-known Japanese comedian, Tokoro Joji. At the end of each spot, Joji would change from one character into

another and then introduce one of our products—an unusual twist for a Japanese ad. Unfortunately, in one of the ads we twisted things a bit too far by having Joji transform himself into a Buddhist monk. The ad evoked outrage on the part of many people and required a published apology to that sect of Buddhists in Japan. I don't know how the monk ad slipped through by our people, but it was a good lesson for us about remembering where we were and to whom we were talking.

About a year after the Buddhist monk fiasco, we again developed an ad campaign for the new made-for-Japan products. The theme, "Kodak is color," involved intriguing images in the primary colors: the blue-suited diver; actors dressed in red and shining fire engines, green objects in nature, and yellow paint swatches. Thompson's idea was innovative stuff for Japanese television, but was still within the bounds of selling mood first, product second.

The length of the commercials for "Kodak is color" would also be innovative. In addition to the standard fifteen-second spot, we planned to create thirty- and sixty-second spots. The sixty-second spots were primarily for the media; we planned to introduce the thirty-second spots during prime time, figuring that since television stations often run ten or more fifteen-second ads together, often repeating the same ad, we could get more mileage out of a single, longer spot.

Finally, we took into account what is known in Japan as the "blue-eyed syndrome." I'm told that the Japanese often tire of seeing everyone on the screen with black hair and brown eyes, and therefore feature Americans, Europeans, and Australians in their ads whenever possible. (Not surprisingly, a major talent industry has sprung up in Japan to handle and recruit non-Japanese people for ads. Many American celebrities have made serious cash by starring in Japanese ads, beginning back in the 1970s with Charles Bronson, who was seen on televisions across the land touting a line of male toiletries. On a less stellar scale, an American friend of my wife was spotted by a talent agency and then convinced to star in an ad for a moving company. After she held a quilt out the window of a house, the announcer intoned that the company would pledge to take the same care with your quilt as it would with the rest of your belongings. I'm not sure that Irma's friend fully appreciated being selected on the basis of looking like a "typical American homemaker," but she got a kick out of the experience and made a few dollars to boot.)

Our storyboards for the "Kodak in color" ad campaign reflected everything we knew about advertising in Japan—from the content to the mixture of Japanese and blond, blue-eyed actors in some of the commercials. All that remained to do before production could begin was sell the concept to headquarters. This turned out to be far more problematic than we thought. The initial response was, "We have perfectly good campaigns that work well everywhere else, from Rochester to Melbourne. Why reinvent the wheel just for Japan?" Finally, after many face-to-face meetings in Rochester between our local advertising managers and corporate advertising people, as well as late phone calls and heavy-duty lobbying, Rochester relented and we received permission to go ahead with our Japanese-style advertising program.

The preview to the media made a terrific splash. Our sixty-second ad, which featured all four primary colors, bent the rules but did so in a way that attracted attention. "Astounding what you've packed into a sixty-second commercial," one of the reporters covering the ad beat

for a major newspaper wrote. The audience at the preview thought the thirty- and fifteen-second spots were big hits, too.

Fortunately, the rest of the country also enjoyed them; within several months after the ad campaign began, our recognition and approval levels had soared to all-time highs. There was still much work to be done in maintaining the turf we'd gained; Fuji would surely be in hot pursuit with an accelerated campaign of its own. But for the time being, we could enjoy our success and savor Kodak's moment under the rising sun.

Nothing moves product in Japan like a demonstration of strong corporate virtues; if you can sell your company, you can sell your product.

AND NOW A WORD FROM OUR SPONSOR

YOU GUYS JUST DON'T TRY HARD ENOUGH
Why There's No Trade Problem Here

"A meeting with the Deputy Minister of Foreign Affairs? You're kidding," Nakano-san, my administrative assistant, said to me incredulously.

"No, it's for real," I respond. "The meeting is set. What a great opportunity for us to talk about our problems with the distribution system."

"Sieg-san, remember an old saying when you're there," another colleague said with a concerned look on his face.

"What's that?"

"The nail that sticks up gets hammered down."

An invitation to meet with the Deputy Minister of Foreign Affairs—the equivalent of visiting the American under Secretary of State—certainly wasn't something you received every day. But we'd worked very hard to get to this point, and I felt optimistic that we might finally get some action on a chief complaint of ours: the fact that Kodak film was not being sold through a major portion of the Japanese distribution system.

The Japanese channels of distribution are part of a complex, multitiered system that spans up to four levels. That means certain products pass through four sets of hands before they're available to the customer. This is particularly true of products sold at small shops and kiosks (which often have no more than six square feet of storage space). In fact, these tiny outlets are often replenished a number of times throughout the day by small trucks or motorbikes that deliver "just-in-time inventory": a small number of magazines, packs of cigarettes, pieces of candy, and say ten rolls of film. Fuji film, that is, and that was the rub for us, especially in the kiosks.

The kiosks have a critical role in the sale of film products in Japan, particularly those located near train stations. These mom-and-pop operations sell a hugely disproportionate amount of film for their size; the Japanese are constantly taking pictures and buying more film, and the kiosk is a favorite place to buy it on the way to work or to a tourist location or recreation spot. So it was with great dismay that we noticed the lack of Kodak film in the twenty kiosks that we surveyed.

The reasons that the kiosks didn't carry Kodak film were pretty clear. When the railroads were owned by the government, its guidelines were that if a product was available nationally, that's what you sold. And none of the kiosk owners were about to complain. The

railroad used the kiosks as a way to give retirees and the families of railway workers who were injured or deceased a means of making a living. So the people who got the rights to operate the kiosks—plum jobs, according to many—were greatly indebted to the national railroads.

When the railroads were privatized in the mid-1980s, and the name changed from Japan National Railroad to Japan Railroad, we thought it would be a good time to try to break into the fourth tier of the distribution system. So we spoke with many kiosk people who informed us that they had no objection to selling Kodak film but that they could sell only what the "guy on the motorcycle brings us. We don't want to upset that system in any way."

Clearly, the situation wasn't going to change, so I brought the matter up with Michael Armacost, U.S. ambassador at the time.

I'd been meeting with Mr. Armacost monthly as a member of the American Chamber of Commerce, which included representatives of *Fortune* 100 companies such as DuPont, Exxon, General Motors, Ford, Caterpillar, Weyerhaeuser, Eastman Kodak, as well as small U.S. companies that had as few as five employees. Mr. Armacost was deeply committed to helping American business thrive in Japan and once told us that he was, in effect, "the first commercial officer of the United States in Japan."

About the time of the change of railway kiosk ownership, Ambassador Armacost was soliciting incidents that documented longstanding complaints from American businessmen about not being able to get into the Japanese distribution system. At one of the monthly meetings we related our inability to get our film into the kiosks, even though we had made pricing offers that should have been hard to refuse. The ambassador took copious notes and promised that he'd take the matter up with the Japanese government.

I was impressed with Mr. Armacost's commitment but was frankly surprised when his secretary called a week later to announce that he'd arranged a meeting for me and my top Japanese executives to meet with the Deputy Minister for Foreign Affairs, Kunihiro-*san*. The minister did not believe that the kiosks refused to carry our film and wanted to discuss the matter in person with us in his office in downtown Tokyo.

Several weeks after the call, I found myself sitting in the Deputy minister's conference room along with my associate Sawada-*san*. A robust, larger-than-average man, Kunihiro-*san* asked us to present our evidence, which I did in English to a translator in the conference room. I was encouraged because Sawada-*san* was with me to make sure that nothing got confused during the translation process.

The kiosk problem was fully described as being a genuine case of a trade barrier established by a long-standing distribution system impervious to change. Because of this trade barrier, we were denying the Japanese public the option of choice.

Kunihiro-*san* nodded when I was done and said he would investigate the matter and get back to us. On the way back Sawada-*san* still couldn't believe that we'd just made a formal complaint to such a high official. Japanese are inherently leery of rocking the boat, even when the cause is just.

Three weeks later, Sawada-*san* and I had an invitation to return to the Deputy Minister's office. When we arrived, we were surprised to find two new people in the conference room, one who was not identified and was taking notes—probably one of the deputy minister's

assistants, I assumed. The other person was introduced as the president of the Japan Railroad kiosk association. Kunihiro-*san* got right down to business, explaining through his translator that he'd sent an associate into the streets to visit "every train station" and check out whether our claim had any validity. He then held up the small yellow box his associate had found in a railroad kiosk, and pointed to it, saying, "I told you that we have no discrimination against foreign products," echoing the sentiment of so many Japanese business leaders and implying that we just don't try hard enough to sell our products in Japan.

I was so flabbergasted that I couldn't respond to the absurdity of the claim. I didn't even recognize the packaging on the box. I suspect that it had been lying around for years as an oddity or collector's item (kiosk owners frequently display "exotic" finds to attract passersby). But even if it was current, which is highly doubtful, one box found among all of the railway kiosks in Tokyo would represent distribution by one-tenth of 1 percent of the potential outlets.

My shock at the response was only amplified the next morning when I received a translation of the article that appeared in the business section of the *Asbai Shinbun*, one of the largest newspapers in Japan. The article explained that contrary to Kodak's complaint about trade barriers, an investigation by the Deputy Minister of Foreign Affairs revealed that it was possible to buy Kodak film at railroad station kiosks.

Apparently, the third face in the deputy minister's office was a reporter from the newspaper. We were set up by the government's efforts to save face in view of its longstanding claim that trade barriers such as the one giving Kodak difficulty simply didn't exist and that the real problem was our lack of perseverance. I felt angry at myself for not asking more about the unidentified party in the room and whether we were engaged in a public meeting. Had I known the fellow was a reporter, I would have made a great effort to establish how many kiosks the minister's assistant actually visited and would have done all I could to have the reporter do his own random study of the kiosks to see how many carried Kodak film.

After three weeks, we met again with the deputy minister, this time to protest in the most polite way possible by listing the most salient points that I thought the reporter had missed. I worked very hard to control my sense of outrage, since this man had enormous sway over foreign businesses, including which ones could operate in his country. Kunihiro-*san* again nodded and said he would look into it.

I left feeling that at least I had a chance to respond to what was clearly a cheap tactic. But over the next year, things did begin to change, and a small but growing number of kiosks began to carry Kodak film, especially those near the *gaijin* areas of Tokyo. Apparently, our meeting with Kunihiro-*san* had set in motion some behind-the-scenes activity that even made it possible to set up a completely Kodak-stocked kiosk in Shinagawa station. Not a bad improvement from the solo roll that the government found just a few years earlier.

Trying harder in Japan means not accepting the status quo;
keep hammering away and the system will eventually begin to
work in your favor.

I COULDN'T HAVE
SAID THAT WHILE
I WAS SOBER

Riding the Last Train from Ginza

"Kompai!" I said as I raised my glass with Chino-san in the club house restaurant. A few more toasts were made as the "awards" were given out for the eighteen holes that a group of executives from his company and Kodak had just played at the course in Suwa City, four hours out of Tokyo. We then dined and talked about the game, and Chino-san suggested that he and I and our translator go out for a private drink at his favorite club.

"Aha," I thought to myself. "Now we're going to get down to business!"

About a year before the golf game, Kodak had taken an equity position in Chinon, Inc., a manufacturer of cameras and computer peripherals. At first things seemed to be going quite well; new products were on track and everyone seemed to be happy. But then we began getting reports "through the grapevine" that the president of Chinon was unhappy with the communication with Kodak and wanted to make a change. But Japanese protocol made it impossible for Chinon's top executive to walk into Kodak and tell me what was wrong; Eastman Kodak was twenty times the size of Chinon, and that established the hierarchical relationship.

"What's the best way to handle this?" I asked my Japanese colleagues.

"Get together for a social occasion," Kimura-*san*, one of our three Japanese presidents, answered.

"Don't tell me," I said with a groan. "Golf."

Kimura-*san* laughed and nodded his head.

Not surprisingly, Chino-*san* was delighted about the idea of our companies sponsoring a golf tournament. I brought several of my top Japanese and American colleagues, and Chino-*san* arrived with his entourage of managers. The game and following dinner were characterized by chitchat and questions about our families and life back in America—the usual warm-up business fare.

Later, Chino-*san* and I went off together to his favorite watering hole (where he had his own private liquor stash), and the waitress brought him his best bottle of scotch. We then talked about what a great day it had been and how terrific the gathering was for relations between the two companies. But there was just one thing that "needed some improvement. . . ." This was the doorway I'd been waiting for,

and during the next twenty minutes we were able to really focus on the communications problems and how we'd resolve them. Then, like a little rift in the social order that had magically healed itself, the conversation drifted back to mundane chat.

The next day, I explained the situation to my Japanese colleagues, and we developed plans for improving the two-way communication links between Chinon and Kodak. Within a few weeks, we heard that everyone was happy, and the case was closed.

Off-line sessions like the one that Chino-*san* and I engaged in are the culturally accepted venue for resolving many types of business issues in Japan. In that way, they reflect the *kata* of "doing business." In Japan, everything has its own *kata* or "proper way of doing things." There's a *kata* of arranging flowers, a *kata* of pouring tea, a *kata* for the way sumo wrestlers conduct their sport. The *kata* are designed to mold young minds and ensure cultural continuity.

The off-line socializing is so important because the way to do business is to avoid causing stress or disharmony in the workplace. It provides a way for subordinates to respond to questions from management without appearing defiant if the answers aren't exactly what management wants to hear. It also offers a way for subordinates to reconcile differences between *tatemae* (the expected truth) and *honne* (the real truth). For instance, a division manager might ask if everyone understands an assignment. Everyone may well say, "Yes, yes, yes." But then nothing will happen, and it will become clear that no one could proceed because there wasn't enough information to go ahead. The subordinates were simply giving the expected answer to maintain harmony within the company. Off-line socializing, which often includes a drink or two, would provide an opportunity for people to express their true feelings that their managers didn't provide enough background information or details for them to do their jobs.

After-hours socializing applies to all sorts of relationships, not just managers and subordinates. The after-hours sessions might include customers, vendors, fellow workers, bankers, and lawyers who work with the company—just about anyone connected in any way to the organization. The topics can range from talking about problems in the office to a new product-development plan to a serious attempt to close a deal with a customer, talk down a supplier on price, or interest a potential joint-venture partner. Coworkers might go out once or twice a week, while sales and marketing people could take customers out three times a week or more. Those who regularly engage in off-line drinking often have private stocks of liquor and a house account, and if you walk into a popular bar in Ginza, you're likely to see rows of bottles bearing people's names on them.

It's safe for people to say what's really on their minds at the bars because of the alcohol, which can transform the normally reticent Japanese into outspoken critics and animated talkers. Nothing says it like the phrase "Shirafu ja ienai" (I could not have said that if I was sober). Even those who are teetotallers and many are (the drinks are often heavily watered down) have the luxury of overstepping their normally reserved selves. Some serious drinking does take place, of course, as a ride on the last train from Ginza reveals (you sometimes have to step over a number of inebriated souls who have somehow made their way back to the train stops).

If people have gone on to a second or third party that won't break up until after the last train, and they have a high enough company position, they'll most likely have a driver waiting for them. Otherwise,

they'll take their chances of finding a cab, or they'll check into a "capsule hotel" and rent a cubbyhole just big enough to stand up in but large enough to have a bed and television. (The capsule hotels are often cheaper than a cab ride. After the trains stop running, the only way that cabs will stop is if you hold up two or three fingers, indicating that you're willing to pay two or three times the normal fare.) Wherever you stayed the night or however you got home, a kind of socially acceptable amnesia sets in the next day and no one will discuss what took place after working hours. But that's the way it's supposed to be; the after-hours socializing serves as a pressure valve for a superstructured workplace. Without it, who knows what might happen during the regular course of business?

Kata is everything; what might seem frivolous on the surface is often critical in maintaining harmony and balance in all realms of life.

EXPLOITING
THE AMERICAN
ACHILLES HEEL

How the Japanese Gain the Upper Hand
in Negotiations

When in a duel, you must forestall the enemy and attack when you have first recognized his school of strategy, perceived his quality, and his strong and weak points. Attack in an unsuspected manner . . . attacking at the weak points and attacking with crushing blows.

—Musashi, The Five Rings (1645)

If Musashi had lived several hundred years later, he probably would have illustrated his classic book of military strategy with copious examples from the world of business. The meetings between Eastman Kodak's copier division and Canon about a proposed alliance would have been a prime candidate for opening the chapter on exploiting an opponent's weakness and then wearing him down.

In the late 1980s, Canon approached us about an idea for an alliance with Eastman Kodak's copier division. The idea made eminently good sense for both parties. Canon needed us because the Fuji-Xerox joint venture was capturing the high-volume copier market. Kodak needed Canon because it wanted to better compete with Xerox in the low-volume end in the United States. And because customers were looking for "complete solutions" to their office needs, it was critical to carry a wide range of copier products from low to high volume.

Specifically, our people in Rochester wanted Canon to agree to sell us product that they would modify to our specifications and that we would sell in our own trade dress. Canon, in return, wanted access to the technology we'd developed for high-volume copying. By sharing technologies and helping each other with manufacturing, the Canon-Kodak alliance would cover the spectrum of copier purchasers and become a potent force in the copier marketplace, creating a win-win situation for both companies.

The basic concept made a lot of sense, so we assumed that ironing out the specifics would be a relatively straightforward process. How wrong we were! At the heart of the problem, the two sides wanted fundamentally different things from the alliance. We saw the alliance as a quick fix for a competitive problem. Canon, not surprisingly, was

looking for a longer relationship that could lead to all sorts of joint projects. Although this hidden agenda never really came out during the negotiations, it undermined our efforts to reach agreement.

The plan called for top people from our Copier Products Division to fly to Japan and meet with the top Canon officials and negotiate an arrangement for products and technology. Kodak Japan's role in this affair was to serve as negotiating coach and to help expedite the deal-making process through off-line communications with Canon's people.

The Copier Division representatives arrived on a Sunday for our first meeting, which was scheduled for the following day. We spent quite a bit of time that night discussing the cultural underpinnings of meetings in Japan and what everyone should expect. I explained the typical protocol for a first Japanese meeting and how you move from general chitchat to the matters at hand—all in good time. "Remember that you're going in to build a relationship," I said.

While the need to "do it their way and in their own time frame" made sense to everyone, we all had been informed by the corporate offices that the marketing gap in our copier line was severe and that we needed to press hard to conclude a deal. Those of us at Kodak Japan were worried that the need to wrap things up would make us look too aggressive and therefore compromise our ability to negotiate effectively. In Musashi's words, we might be forced to reveal one of our major weaknesses.

The first meeting was held at Canon's headquarters in Tokyo and began with the obligatory discussion about family and golf. The Kodak people did fairly well at playing the game. Then Canon made a presentation about its technology, and Kodak did the same, although to Kodak, none of the information was terribly new or exciting. Only hints were made about each company's business strategy in the copier marketplace and what it hoped to receive from the alliance. The vice president of Canon then adjourned the meeting for the day and said how much he was looking forward to our next session, which would be held at Kodak's offices.

As soon as we walked out the door, two of our copier people couldn't suppress their frustrations any longer. "Al, you've got to do something," one of them blurted out in the cab. "Tell 'em to stop wasting our time. We didn't fly almost six thousand miles to listen to this kind of lightweight stuff that could have been easily done with a phone call."

"Look," I said, "it might not seem like much is happening, but believe me, we're under the microscope. This afternoon they were simply tossing out bits of information to gauge your reaction. They're incredibly adept at watching body language; they probably weren't even listening to what you were saying—they were just assessing our strengths and weaknesses. They also realize that when five people come over from Rochester for a meeting there's likely to be a hidden player who has more power than the others, and they're trying to figure out who that person might be."

Still, to make the Rochester contingent feel better, I assured them that some people from my office would hold some off-line discussions with the Canon people and see if they couldn't move things along a bit.

At the second meeting, we did make some forward movement, probably because a few of my people got together with their Canon counterparts. But the progress wasn't nearly enough to satisfy our people from Rochester, who at this point just wanted to sit down with

Canon's engineers and talk about the details of the arrangement. At each request for specificity, the Japanese simply remained vague and asked lots of questions, many of them appearing tangential to the Rochester contingent.

The meeting adjourned again with the people from Rochester trying to figure out if they were going to leave with a deal in hand. I was straightforward with them and warned them about pushing too hard: in tomorrow's meeting that would just weaken our position. "If they know that you have to be at Narita airport for a five o'clock plane, and they know that you really want to conclude a deal so you can return to Rochester with something to lay out for the Copier Division's management, you'll be in a pretty poor position to get what you want. Relax."

At the third meeting the copier people laid out exactly what they wanted, which I'm sure was perceived as a challenge. One member of the Canon negotiating team nodded his head and said, "We understand what you want. Thank you very much. We will give it very serious consideration. And we will get back to you." There was total silence until the end of the meeting, when it was time to send my U.S. colleagues back to the airport.

As we were waiting in the lobby of the Canon office building for our cars to arrive, I tried to review what had happened and to stress that our series of meetings was not a failure just because we didn't conclude with a formal agreement that both parties accepted. I didn't think it was the best time to mention *how* many more meetings I thought it would take to close the deal (about a dozen in total, I figured), but I advised them that we were only at the beginning of what would likely be a longer-term process.

"This is a land where people have extraordinary patience," I explained. "They're willing to wait twenty-five years for a membership in the most popular tennis clubs, and they take out sixty-year mortgages. So what's a few extra meetings during the normal course of business? Besides, from a negotiating standpoint, they know that Americans are very impatient people who need to wrap things up as quickly as possible. And they know that if you keep coming back empty-handed, you'll get even more anxious because you'll worry about your boss questioning whether you're the right guy to make the deal happen. The more anxious you get, the more you'll be willing to give up. If you don't want to give away the store, you've got to play it their way."

The exhausted copier team went back to Rochester looking worse for wear, but did return to Japan several times during the next six months. In addition, there were many questions about the deal that went back and forth across the Pacific by fax.

Canon people also went to Rochester several times. A year later, a member of the office of the chairman in Rochester came to Tokyo to shake hands with the president of Canon, acknowledging that the beginnings of an alliance had been put in place, and the particulars of the deal we'd been negotiating had been agreed to. And all this happened in just ten meetings!

As Musashi advises, never try to move strong things by pushing directly. Instead, take advantage of all the weaknesses you can find.

SAYONARA
Passing the Reins on to a Successor

"It's your turn to talk now, Sieg-san," Hioki-san said to me at the beginning of my farewell party in the grand ballroom of the Laforet Hotel. "This will be your last big speech in Japanese. That must make you happy!"

In fact, I was relieved at the thought of not having to make another public oration in what had become my quasi-second language. But I still felt a lump in my throat as I got up to officially say goodbye to so many people who had become my friends and loyal colleagues. When I finished the Japanese version, I repeated it in English for my Western colleagues (about thirty in total). Two hours later I was whisked off to a second party at a karaoke bar (I wasn't asked to sing, even on this special occasion), then on to a yakatori bar for some late-night chicken snacks. To this day I'm not sure what time I returned home that night.

In the United States, when you feel it's time to move on to the next stage of your career, you can pretty much clean out your office and leave two or three weeks after announcing your plans. You can leave even sooner if you have a good reason to, and chances are that you won't disrupt the inner workings of the company. As the top executive of a foreign company in Japan, though, I knew that I couldn't simply pass on the torch. One of the main assets I'd developed for the company during my stay was a set of close personal relationships with our bankers, lawyers, mini-*keiretsu* associates, joint-venture partners, vendors, and, of course, our customers.

Strong relationship capital is not easily transferrable, so I insisted that my successor, Bob Smith, a business unit manager and vice president from Rochester, as well as a former manager of our Latin American region, join me six months before my departure. My reasoning took a bit of explaining, but Bob did show up six months before he was to take the helm of Kodak Japan, and we spent a great deal of time going to lunches, dinners, and parties with key Japanese players so that I could make personal introductions and an appeal that they give him the same support that they'd given me. We also spent a surprising amount of time taking care of governmental and legal issues surrounding the transfer of executive power; when we got down to the final few weeks, the logistics of the move reached a fever pitch.

Tidying up my own personal affairs and sending our belongings back to Rochester was no small task either; although our house was much smaller than our dwelling in Rochester, we'd managed to accumulate an amazing amount of goods (I joked to Irma that if we stayed any longer, we could have singlehandedly taken care of the trade imbalance).

The final days before my departure were punctuated by at least twenty-five parties thrown on my behalf by vendors, customers, and business associates. But the Kodak Japan party would be the penultimate goodbye event, in terms of the size and the closeness of the colleagues who'd be attending. I'd attended so many parties during the past seven years that it didn't really hit me that this was *my* swan song until I walked into the hotel lobby and saw a sign that read, "*Sayonara Party of Sieg*." After speeches on my behalf, and my own parting words, my Japanese colleagues presented me with a magnificent 400-year-old wood-block print beautifully framed in lacquered spruce. Today, this incredible memory of my Japan experience hangs proudly as the centerpiece of our living room.

Two days after the farewell party, Irma and I made our last official trip to Narita airport, following a tearful early morning send-off by several close friends. It wasn't until the wheels of the plane nestled into the wings that I began thinking about the fact that I was no longer Sieg from Kodak Japan; I'd turned in my alien registration certificate, multiple reentry permit, and other official papers. I *was* really leaving Japan, although not quite for home: we thought we'd take a real vacation in Australia before acclimatizing ourselves to life back in the United States. (Besides, Irma wanted to go where we could "drink the water and understand the language." The water part was no problem; the language, however, was often inscrutable to us.)

As the plane reached cruising altitude and we settled in for the eight-hour flight to Cairns, we began talking about some of the most important things we'd learned and about the misconceptions that we'd brought with us from the States. We were both impressed by the warmth of the Japanese people, despite their outward appearance of

being reserved. They really do have a fond feeling for Americans, although they have no particular cravings to *be* Americans. They take the best from our culture (and every other of the world) and "Japanify" it so that it meets their needs. It's easy to confuse the adoption of so many Western trappings with a longing to be "more like us."

We were both impressed by how safe we felt anywhere we went in the country. All three of our daughters lived with us at one time or another during our stay, and we never had any qualms when they toured the streets of Tokyo at night. There aren't too many places you can say that about in the world these days.

We learned a lot about patience, too, from many different sources. We recalled, with a laugh, the time shortly after arriving when we looked out the window one Saturday morning and saw Mt. Fuji, clear as a bell. We'll hop in the car, we thought, and beat the crowds, we naively thought! Three hours later, we were still in Tokyo. So we turned around, went home, then caught a train to Kamakura, a beautiful town on the Pacific Ocean known for its spectacular beaches and temples.

As a player in the Japanese businessworld, I also had many opportunities to learn about patience—at the bargaining table, with our bankers, lawyers, vendors, and business colleagues. Perhaps my biggest lesson, though, concerned new ways of thinking and problem solving. I arrived with the implicit understanding that you get from *A* to *B* to *C* in a linear fashion. But I discovered that "fuzzy logic," with its iterative feedback loops, is equally valid and can lead to exciting breakthroughs in process and quality. I resolved to instill this form of thinking in my associates back in Rochester and expected to reap tremendous rewards in terms of better strategies for the company.

I never really had a chance to sell fuzzy logic at home, though, because of an unexpected offer for early retirement just seven months after I began my new job as Director of Strategic Resources: the numbers were too attractive to pass up. For the next six months I worked on remodeling the house, caught up on reading, and pursued my hobby of nature photography (including a long-hoped-for trip to Katami Peninsula in Alaska to photograph grizzly bears while they fished for salmon).

But my mind kept drifting back to Japan, particularly on how I could use my knowledge and experience to help U.S. firms overcome their fears about doing business there and how they can succeed with good old hard work and American ingenuity. I accepted some offers to lecture and give seminars and then found myself in the consulting business after a few companies invited me to help them maximize their business relationships in Japan. The consulting business not only proved to be my second calling, but it gave me an excuse to visit Tokyo and my old friends.

On the return flight from my first trip back to Japan since turning over the operation to Bob Smith two years earlier, I reminisced about all the changes that had taken place in such a short amount of time, largely because the economic bubble that had been growing for the previous decade finally burst. And when it did, the shock waves reverberated throughout Japanese society. One look at the Ginza with all of the boarded up bars and cabarets said it all. As businesses struggled for the first time since World War II, they began drastically cutting expenses. Also for the first time in recent Japanese history, lifetime employment could no longer be considered a guarantee. College grads—even those from Tokyo U, who used to have four or

five options—suddenly had to compete for jobs as companies began allowing attrition to occur without full replacement.

Troubles in big business quickly trickled down to small business. The recession in the Japanese economy nearly wiped out the entertainment business in Ginza as large firms pulled in their belts. The effects of the belt-tightening also trickled down to the ranks of mom-and-pop operations that support big business. Before the recession, many big businesses found it a cost-effective strategy to farm out a substantial amount of piecemeal work to smaller companies (Toyota, for example, retained the services of scores of small tool and die makers). But when the economy soured, many large firms pulled the work in-house to maximize their internal resources. As a result, an enormous number of small businesses declared bankruptcy.

For U.S. and other foreign firms, the recovery will open some interesting possibilities. As more Japanese begin to accept the idea of paying lower prices and forgoing top-flight service, American companies that understand discounting will be in an excellent position to make inroads into the Japanese marketplace and skirt many of the multitiered distribution hurdles that have made it so difficult for Western companies to do business with Japan in the past.

The recovery period also opens the possibility of doing more direct business with *keiretsu* members. Because of the plummet in the stockmarket, many *keiretsu* members have bought back their cross-shares, which had previously served as a kind of glue that holds the business associations together. While the *keiretsu* are not about to go away and still wield a tremendous amount of power, weakening bonds will likely enable Western firms to find more willing and able partners for alliances and joint ventures. It seems that not a day goes by without

some mention in the U.S. business press of a merger deal or an alliance between American and Japanese companies. In fact, for the first time, mergers and acquisitions may become an accepted way of doing business in Japan.

The drop in land prices also bodes well for Western companies doing business in Japan. Foreign firms will still have to prove that they're committed to the Japanese marketplace before the Japanese bureaucracy will allow them to buy land. But falling prices can only open more options for Western businesses that need to break ground for manufacturing plants and R&D centers.

Finally, in the coming years, *gaijin* firms will have less difficulty attracting Japanese employees. Some Japanese today speak of the *shinjinrui*—the younger generation, which is simply "out for the money" and doesn't care where it comes from. Even so, the concept of lifetime employment will no doubt remain an ideal and will still drive many people to seek jobs at the largest Japanese firms. But the harsh realities of Japan's new economy will likely lead many Japanese people to reconsider the possibilities of working for *gaijin* companies.

While potential opportunities might be just around the corner, U.S. firms would do well not to get too complacent; Japan's resiliency should never be underestimated. Despite the reductions in income, due to bonus reductions (Japanese employees traditionally receive summer and year-end bonuses), the rate of savings in Japan is still 14 to 18 percent—which is four to five times higher than in the United States. That means there's still a tremendous amount of liquidity and plenty of funds available to support a revitalized Japanese economy. And large Japanese firms, because of their downsizing through

attrition, will emerge from the recession lean and strong and more competitive than ever.

Japan has recovered from many crises since World War II, including the Nixon soybean embargo of 1970, the oil shocks of 1973 and 1977, and the yen shock of 1985. With the yen achieving parity in 1994, Japanese firms are scrambling to cut costs even further in order to achieve their financial projections.

If history repeats itself, Japan will emerge from the current economic crises ready to adopt a leadership stance; few people doubt that it will be a driving force in the rise to power of the Asian "tigers." Driven by *ichiban* (the work ethic that exhorts individuals and organizations to do their best) and an innate sense of how to leverage group brainpower, Japan can count on tremendous support from its workforce to sustain the recovery. And fueled by the relentless drive to be number one, you can be sure that Japan will resume the game of "Business *Go*" with the fury of a tidal wave.

When leaving for good, say "Sayonara." When making a temporary exit, say "Ja mata"—I'll see you again.

ABOUT THE AUTHORS

Albert Sieg

Albert L. Sieg served with Eastman Kodak Company for thirty-seven years, entering as a research chemist and retiring as a corporate vice president and Director of Strategic Resources. He holds a Ph.D. in organic chemistry from the University of Rochester and completed the Program for Management Development at the Graduate School of Business at Harvard University. During his last seven years with the company, Dr. Sieg served as the president of Eastman Kodak (Japan), a wholly owned subsidiary based in Tokyo. Under Dr. Sieg's direction, Eastman Kodak (Japan) grew from a fledgling eleven-person operation to a serious contender in the Japanese photographic marketplace with more than 4,000 employees. After returning from Japan, he established a consulting practice designed to help companies establish operations and build a presence in the Asian-Pacific marketplace. Between consulting assignments, Dr. Sieg, an avid professional nature

photographer, travels the world in search of grizzly bears, harp seal pups, and other wildlife subjects. He lives in Rochester, New York, with his wife, Irma.

Steven J. Bennett

Steven J. Bennett is a full-time author who has written more than fifty books on business, the environment, computing, and parenting. He worked with Stephen Frangos on *Team Zebra: How 1500 Partners Revitalized Eastman Kodak's Black & White Film-Making Flow* (Omneo/Oliver Wight). He holds a master's degree in East Asian studies from Harvard University and lives with his family in Cambridge, Massachusetts.